THIS BOOK WILL REKINDLE YOUR HOPE.

RENE E SWOPE, bestselling author of *A Confident Heart*

# Real-Life

## ROMANCE

INSPIRING STORIES
TO HELP YOU
BELIEVE IN
TRUE LOVE

*Rhonda Stoppe*

## Acknowledgments

With all my heart I thank each and every couple who peeled back the pages of their own lives to share their stories. Your consent to make yourselves vulnerable by revealing how your love survived through deep sorrow and regret is what makes this book an incredible resource to help any couple discover the secret to building a marriage with no regrets.

Our sweet church family at First Baptist Church of Patterson, California, I am grateful for you all. Your prayer support and encouragement are the strength behind this project. Thank you for loving us well and for joining with us in serving our Savior.

To each of my children and their spouses, your love for each other rooted and grounded in God's perfect love is a source of great joy and inspiration for your father and me. We pray God continues to knit together your hearts in love for Christ and in love for each other so that your love is the light He will use to draw many—including your children—to the hope of Jesus Christ.

Steve, my incredible husband, thank you for loving me well. And thank you for letting me lock myself away to write this book. I know the sacrifices you make to allow me to write, and for that I am grateful. You're my favorite!

Special thanks to my editor, Kathleen. Your amazing insight and inspiration is what has made this book a timeless treasure to be passed down for generations to come.

*Notes*

## CHAPTER 3: WAITING ON GOD'S TIMING

1. Boundless.org is a community for Christian young adults who want to grow up, own their faith, date with purpose, and prepare for marriage.
2. Suzanne Hadley Gosselin, "A Year to Love," *Boundless,* July 15, 2009, http://www.Boundless.org/relationships/2009/a-year-to-love.

## CHAPTER 12: ADDICTED TO EACH OTHER

1. To learn more about Jesus's saving grace, please read *How to Have a Relationship with Jesus* on page 231 of this book.

## CHAPTER 14: SURPRISED BY LOVE

1. You can hear this podcast yourself at http://www.engagingstory.com/stories/.

## CHAPTER 15: CONNECTED AT THE HEART

1. More help to build a No Regrets Marriage can be found in Rhonda's book, *The Marriage Mentor* (Eugene, OR: Harvest House Publishers, 2018).

## CHAPTER 17: FROM HOPELESS TO HOPEFUL

1. Nicola Menzie, "Nick Vujicic's Wife, Kanae, Tells of 'Magical' Moment They First Locked Eyes in 'Love Without Limits'" (Part 2), *The Christian Post*, November 29, 2014: http://www.christianpost.com/news/nick-vujicics-wife-kanae-tells-of-magical-moment-they-first-locked-eyes-in-love-without-limits-part-2-130417/#eXEFcz7i0A3WyZDD.99.
2. Parts of this story were gathered from Paula John, "The Beautiful Love Story of Nick Vujicic and His Wife Kanae Miyahara," Part 1, *The Christian Post* http://ipost.christianpost.com/post/the-beautiful-love-story-of-nick-vujicic-and-his-wife-kanae-miyahara; Nicola Menzie, "Nick Vujicic's Wife, Kanae, Tells of 'Magical' Moment They First Locked Eyes in Love Without Limits" Part 2, *The Christian Post:* http://www.christianpost.com/news/nick-vujicics-wife-kanae-tells-of-magical-moment-they-first-locked-eyes-in-love-without-limits-part-2-130417/#eXEFcz7i0A3WyZDD.99; and iPost: http://ipost.christianpost.com/post/the-beautiful-love-story-of-nick-vujicic-and-his-wife-kanae-miyahara.

## CHAPTER 20: UNTIL THE FINAL BREATH

1. Rhonda and Steve Stoppe speak together at their NoRegretsMarriage conferences.

## CHAPTER 24: THE SURPRISE WEDDING

1. Rhonda Stoppe, *Moms Raising Sons to Be Men* (Eugene, OR: Harvest House, 2013), 103.

## CHAPTER 25: COURAGEOUS LOVE

1. Eusebius Pahmphilus, *Eusebius' Ecclesiastical History* (Grand Rapids, MI: Baker, 1974), 115-16.
2. The apostle Peter's love story taken from: Rhonda Stoppe, *If My Husband Would Change I'd Be Happy* (Eugene, OR: Harvest House 2016), 193-94.

## What People Are Saying
## About *Real-Life Romance*

Ever wonder if a Christ-centered romance is possible? This book is filled with real-life stories that will rekindle your hope and remind you how good God is at writing the best love stories!

~**Renee Swope,** bestselling author of *A Confident Heart*

Everyone loves love. And even more so, we love a great love story! In *Real-Life Romance*, we hear and see how God weaves hearts and lives together to create something amazing! If you are wondering what's next in life or in love, turn the pages of this book, and let the love God has for you infuse love into your relationship.

~**Pam Farrel,** author of 45 books including *Men Are Like Waffles,
Women Are Like Spaghetti* and *Red Hot Monogamy*

How do men and women fall in love? Their stories are as unique as the couples themselves, yet as we see in *Real-Life Romance* true love not only brings couples together, but also can guide them to true satisfaction in God. If you've been heartbroken by marriages that don't last, be encouraged by this book. True love is possible, even for fallible humans. It's inspiring to read about how God still works in real lives, real marriages!

~**Tricia Goyer,** author of 70 books, including *Walk It Out*

You will laugh, cry, and be challenged by this wonderful book. In a masterful way, Rhonda shares the real-life stories of many different couples. She lets us look inside each relationship at the life-changing challenges they face. Each story is filled with hope, as we see God act in amazing ways. Throughout the book, it is clear that the greatest romance of all is His amazing love for us.

~**Kim Kimberling, PhD,** Founder of the Awesome Marriage
Movement and author of *7 Secrets to an Awesome Marriage*

*Real-Life Romance* feels like a coffee date with Rhonda. This isn't just another book about marriage; instead, Rhonda's girlfriend-like voice makes her writing feel as though she's talking straight to you, offering the hope that Jesus brings when you trust Him with your love life.

~**Melissa Hightower,** International Moms Ministry Community Coach

*Real-Life Romance* is a breath of fresh air. Rhonda's uplifting "real-life" stories remind us that we each have our own story. Every marriage starts with a love story, although we tend to forget it and get swept away with the mundane of life after "I do." Rhonda masterfully turns our focus and attention back to the One who created marriage and to His Word. This book is a must-read for those needing encouragement in their marriage.

~**Kristi Clover,** author, speaker, host of the Simply Joyful Podcast

*Real-Life Romance* is an easy-to-read book for the mom on the go. Within minutes of reading, this book will captivate your heart, and you will want to find more time to read and connect with this truly amazing author. Through the love stories she shares, you will find yourself falling in love again and again, one story at a time!

~**Yesenia Jamison,** Financial Coordinator & MOPs Kids Coordinator, Big Valley Grace Community Church, Modesto, CA

I loved reading *Real-Life Romance*! It showed me that every love story is uniquely fashioned by God. I especially enjoyed where Rhonda, from a mom's perspective, shares the love stories of her own children. Rhonda inspires me to be a mentor to young married and single woman using *Real-Life Romance* as a resource. This book will help you put Christ first in your romance, rediscover passion in your marriage, and record your love story for the next generation.

~**Becca Mundt,** Engaging Story podcast host

# Real-Life ROMANCE

Rhonda Stoppe

**HARVEST HOUSE PUBLISHERS**
EUGENE, OREGON

## REAL-LIFE ROMANCE
Copyright © 2018 Rhonda Stoppe
Published by Harvest House Publishers
Eugene, Oregon 97408
www.harvesthousepublishers.com

ISBN 978-0-7369-7141-6 (pbk.)
ISBN 978-0-7369-7142-3 (eBook)

Library of Congress Cataloging-in-Publication Data

Names: Stoppe, Rhonda, 1961- author.
Title: Real-life romance / Rhonda Stoppe.
Description: Eugene, Oregon : Harvest House Publishers, [2018] | Includes
    bibliographical references.
Identifiers: LCCN 2017023230 (print) | LCCN 2017039980 (ebook) | ISBN
    9780736971423 (ebook) | ISBN 9780736971416 (pbk.)
Subjects: LCSH: Love—Religious aspects--Christianity. | Man-woman
    relationships—Religious aspects—Christianity.
Classification: LCC BV4639 (ebook) | LCC BV4639 .S76 2018 (print) | DDC
    241/.4—dc23
LC record available at https://lccn.loc.gov/2017023230

**Printed in the United States of America**

17 18 19 20 21 22 23 24 25 26 / BP-SK / 10 9 8 7 6 5 4 3 2 1

To Steve Stoppe—the love of my life

The mystery of lifelong love—the treasure that we share
To walk life's path in the shadows of your kind and tender care

How good is God to give me you so many years ago
The depth and width of our love that only He could grow

Who could have dreamt this height of love that we could e'er achieve
Yet not our strength but His alone has caused us to believe

The story of us—my favorite tale of a love so true
Oh for a thousand lifetimes to be in love with you

*Soli Deo Gloria*

# Contents

Introduction . . . . . . . . . . . . . . . . . . . . . . . . . . . . . . . . 9

1. When God Writes Your Love Story—Steve and Rhonda . . 11

2. A Lifelong Love—John and Denel . . . . . . . . . . . . . . . . 25

3. Waiting on God's Timing—Kevin and Suzanne . . . . . . 33

4. The Heart's True Desire—Jason and Noelle . . . . . . . . . 39

5. The Way Christ Forgives—Nate and Jillian . . . . . . . . . 47

6. A Kiss Will Only Complicate Things—James and Missy . . 53

7. The Single-Parent Club—Matt and Dawn . . . . . . . . . . 63

8. A Time to Grow—Sean and Allison . . . . . . . . . . . . . . . 71

9. Dreams Don't Come True for a Girl Like Me
   —Byron and Tammy . . . . . . . . . . . . . . . . . . . . . . . 79

10. The Secret—Chuck and Angie . . . . . . . . . . . . . . . . . . . 85

11. Love Survives Loss—Don and Barb . . . . . . . . . . . . . . . 97

12. Addicted to Each Other—Jeff and Jennifer . . . . . . . . 105

13. The Perfect Husband—Josh and Julie . . . . . . . . . . . . 115

14. Surprised by Love—Matt and Becca . . . . . . . . . . . . . 125

15. Connected at the Heart—Bill and Pam . . . . . . . . . . . 131

16. A Chance Encounter—James and Valder . . . . . . . . . . 141

17. From Hopeless to Hopeful—Nick and Kanae . . . . . . 147

18. Happily Ever After...Again—Walter and Sandy . . . . . 153

19. Something Set Apart—Steve and Becky . . . . . . . . . . . 161

20. Until the Final Breath—Curt and Vi . . . . . . . . . . . . . 169

21. Breaking the Bro Code—Estevan and Kayla . . . . . . . . 177

22. She Feels Like Home—Brandon and Jessy . . . . . . . . . . 189

23. Turning to Each Other in Trial—Jake and Meredith . . 197

24. The Surprise Wedding—Tony and Kylene . . . . . . . . . . 209

25. Courageous Love—The Apostle Peter and His Wife . . 219

26. One Last Love Story . . . . . . . . . . . . . . . . . . . . . . . . . . . 225

Epilogue . . . . . . . . . . . . . . . . . . . . . . . . . . . . . . . . . . . . 229

How to Have a Relationship with Jesus . . . . . . . . . . . 231

Notes . . . . . . . . . . . . . . . . . . . . . . . . . . . . . . . . . . . . . . 237

# Introduction

I love watching two people fall in love—don't you? Looking back over Steve's and my love story and recalling all the sweet details of watching my own children fall in love will forever be some of the greatest treasures I keep in the recesses of my mind.

Why do love stories draw us in? I think it's because we each long for our own happily ever after, and if you're a mom you pray for your children to find lifelong love. Love stories give us hope and inspire us to believe that true love—forever love—not only exists but is alive and well in average couples whose depth of love makes them anything but average.

The pages of this book are filled with accounts of how God providentially brought together two hearts to intertwine so completely that their love stands firm. You'll see how, from the highest heights to the deepest sorrows, true love shines brightly in lifelong love. And you'll discover how God's plan is for couples to love each other so deeply with His love that their marriage becomes a light He can use to draw others to know Him.

*Love stories give us hope and inspire us to believe that true love—forever love—not only exists but is alive and well in average couples whose depth of love makes them anything but average.*

Whether you are married, divorced, widowed, or single, this book will meet you where you are and fill you with hope and inspiration. The real-life accounts of the couples in this book will give you hope for your own happily ever after—and for that of your children and grandchildren.

Let it be said of us that our love stood the test of time. Let our children and our grandchildren tell our true love stories for generations to come. Let your story and mine find a place in history as inspiring accounts of real-life romance.

—

### THERE'S MORE!

It's fun to put a face to each story, so in this book I've included a photograph of each couple whose story I tell. And it can be even more fun to connect with the couples as they tell their stories themselves, so don't miss out on the special feature that goes along with this book. Go to my website, NoRegretsWoman.com, to watch or listen to many of the couples in this book talk about how they fell in love.

# 1

# When God Writes Your Love Story

## Steve and Rhonda

JPlazaPhotography

D on't you just love a good love story? I know I do. And my absolute favorite love story of all time is the one God wrote when He knit my heart together with the heart of my husband, Steve, the absolute love of my life. Here's how it all began.

Steve was just 17 years old when he went away to college. His mom had always prayed for him to grow up to be a pastor, so his parents were elated when he decided to attend a Bible college in Denver. While at school, Steve's professors taught him apologetics, Greek, and theology. But the late nights he spent in discussions with the seminary students ignited a passion for God's Word and stirred a desire in his heart to one day become a pastor.

For Steve, college wasn't all about academics. He had a lot of fun in those days. Living near the Rocky Mountains, he learned to mountain climb and rappel down the face of cliffs. If an adventure was to be had, Steve was always game.

The school had many great girls too. He dated some, but his favorite memory is how each weekend he and his friend would invite all the girls who didn't have dates to join them for ice cream in the park. The girls without dates had so much fun that soon many of the girls who could have had dates chose to hang out with their group instead of joining the usual dating scene.

Over time one girl captured Steve's affections. The more time he spent with her, the more he thought maybe she would be the one he would marry. Steve grew to care for her deeply. However, something in his spirit kept him from committing to her. Whenever he considered "forever" with her, he felt conflicted.

Steve wrestled with his lack of peace until he could no longer ignore the conviction in his heart. He knew he had to end the relationship. Although that was difficult, Steve chose to obey the Spirit's leading and do what he knew was right.

Not long after the break up, Steve decided to move so he could be near his parents. They had relocated to a new town while he was away at school, and when he walked into their church, you can imagine how much attention the new guy received from the women in the college group. "Fresh meat" is what I liked to call it. In young adult ministries, the number of eligible women often outnumbers the number of male marriage prospects. Steve, who was quite handsome and a super fun guy, realized an immediate popularity among the women his age.

I attended the Christian high school on the campus where Steve and his family attended church. I was just shy of 15 the day I first met Steve. From the moment I saw him, I had an instant crush. His laugh and smile took my breath away. Secretly, I wished I was closer to his age so he might notice me.

Steve soon began teaching a Bible class at the middle school, and I would occasionally catch glimpses of him on campus. The church also hired him to maintain the buses they used for their outreach ministries. Back in the 1970s, it was common for churches to own a fleet of buses they sent out to bring children to church each Sunday.

One April afternoon my mother came to the school to pick up the kids in our carpool. After waiting on my sister, who had not shown up, my mom asked me to find her. My sister was dating Steve's younger brother, so I knew they were likely together. I headed to the other side of the parking lot where the church buses were parked and repaired. There, with his head underneath the hood of a bus, was Steve.

"Hi. Excuse me. I'm looking for my sister," I said.

"Your sister who?" he teased.

*When God Writes Your Love Story*     13

"My sister who is dating your brother."

"My brother who?"

Now, I knew he had only one brother, but the more I pressed to find out if he had seen my sister, the more playfully he responded without giving me any real answer. At this point I was getting a bit exasperated. My mother had already been waiting in the car for quite some time.

Finally I said, "Obviously you're not gonna help me. I gotta go."

Steve laughed as I moved on.

But then the strangest thing happened. As I walked away from one of the handsomest faces I had ever laid eyes on, I had a fleeting thought: *I'm gonna marry him.* The thought caught me off guard—and embarrassed me. Here I was six years younger than Steve. Why on earth would I even think he would take notice of me, the teenage girl in her brown maxi skirt and velour hoodie?

Steve and I became friends as we chaperoned our siblings' dates. But when they broke up, Steve and I had no reason to see each other socially. I did see him at church, always painfully aware of other young women vying for his attention. I saw less and less of him, until the night I arrived at a high school basketball game in my cheerleader uniform, ready to cheer on our school's team.

I immediately saw Steve's car in the parking lot. He drove an awesome Mediterranean blue Mach 1. The car had a unique gold stripe along the side, so I knew without a doubt it was his. My heart skipped a beat when I realized the opposing team was Steve's alma mater. This was their homecoming game, and Steve would likely be playing in the alumni exhibition.

The prospect of seeing Steve sent my excitement level soaring. He was dribbling a basketball toward me as I walked into the gymnasium. After he went for a layup and made the basket, our eyes met. It was like a moment frozen in time. A moment I'll never forget. As our eyes locked, Steve paused, smiled, gave me a wink, and then ran back down the court to catch up with his teammates.

I thought, *I could die. I could just die! He saw me. There's no doubt he saw me. I'm sure he'll come and find me after the game.*

When Steve's alumni game ended, I was on my side of the gym

getting ready to cheer for our team. When he came out of the locker room, I got butterflies in my stomach. As I was rehearsing in my mind some clever thing I might say to him when we talked, I saw him meet up with a young woman. As she put her arm in his and he escorted her across the gymnasium floor and up into the bleachers, my heart sank. Watching Steve introduce this young woman to his old high school friends in the bleachers was almost too much for me to bear.

I looked down to keep from bursting into tears, and I noticed my young self dressed in cheer attire. *He is never going to notice you. You're just far too young for him.*

Cheering that night wasn't easy. As far as I could tell, Steve never looked at me during the entire event. When the game was over, he left with the other girl—without so much as a nod my way.

## MOVING ON

My crush on Steve did not keep me from liking other boys while I was in high school. I liked one boy very much. I'll call him Tim. I think, however, I was more attracted to how cute Tim was and how much other girls would have liked to date him rather than to who he really was as a person.

Tim wasn't much of a talker, so we spent more time in activities and watching movies than we did conversing. I remember being torn. I loved the idea of being with Tim, but I ached to have someone who wanted to know me and who would share with me from the depths of his heart.

I also knew I wanted to one day marry a man who loved Christ, and while Tim claimed to be a Christian, he rarely spoke of his love for the Lord or any aspirations to serve Him.

In the meantime, my father hired Steve to come to our home to work on one of our cars. (Steve's father owned an auto repair shop, so Steve had grown up working on cars.) I was excited to see him whenever he came, but I was convinced he would never be attracted to someone as young as me. Even so, as Steve spent time working on the car, I often joined him in the garage to talk to him while he worked.

One day I went out to see Steve and Tim standing shoulder to shoulder and having some sort of discussion. You could have cut the tension with a knife. To this day I'm not sure what they talked about, but by his body language, I could see Steve did not approve of this guy who had come to pick me up for a date.

Spending time with Tim definitely wore down my resolve to remain sexually pure until marriage. I never had sex with him, but I do remember one night when the two of us were kissing in my parents' living room after everyone else had gone to bed (unbeknownst to my mom and dad). When the kissing started going further than I wanted it to, I prayed silently, *Oh God, please help me. I don't know how to stop this before it goes too far.*

Just then the telephone in my bedroom rang. I scrambled to answer it before it woke my parents. It was Steve Stoppe!

He said, "Hi. Whatcha doin'?"

"Hi. Noooothing..."

"Are you alone?"

"No."

Then he inquired if I was with the young man I'd been dating and if my parents were awake. When Steve learned that Tim and I were alone in the other room he discerned my situation and said, "I want you to just stay here on the phone with me until he cools off."

I felt like my knight in shining armor had just ridden up on a white horse. Steve had responded to the gentle nudge of the Holy Spirit to call me that night. Little did he know he was protecting the purity of the woman who would one day be his wife!

Steve and I chatted a bit, and after I thought the boy had likely gone home, we said our good-byes.

When I returned to the living room, I was surprised to see Tim still there. "That was Stoppe, wasn't it?"

"Yes, it was."

"You don't want to see me anymore, do you?"

Relieved that he had the insight to bring it up, I said, "No. I don't want to see you anymore."

## WHEN THINGS GOT REAL

I wish now that I had kept a diary of the timeline of events when Steve and I began to fall in love. He spent much time trying to stay clear of the "little girl" who had captured his attention, and I spent just as much time trying to devise ways for our paths to cross so we could enjoy a casual chat.

When speaking to young women at college events, I joke that back in those days, when you wanted to stalk someone, you had to actually stalk them! We had no cell phones and no Internet. You had to figure out where the person was going to be at a certain time and then appear to coincidentally show up at the same location.

One tact I used to see Steve was offering to help him grade papers for the middle school Bible class he taught. Another time I helped him plan a surprise party for his brother's birthday.

Then one day Steve pulled up to our house in his Mach 1. The car made a low rumbling noise as it came up the street, and I remember how my heart would skip a beat whenever I heard that sound. On this day I was a bit more excited since it had been quite a while since I had seen Steve.

I walked outside to greet him before he even got out of his car. He had a CB radio, and I jumped into the passenger seat to listen to him finish up a conversation he was having on the radio. (If you're under the age of thirty, I'm sure you're shocked to think we could get along without cell phones in our cars. But somewhere between the invention of telegrams and this generation with cell phones was the era of CB radios. Truck drivers had always used them, but in the late seventies they had become a fun way to meet people and talk to friends while traveling.)

As I sat in Steve's car, I saw a letter tucked up in the windshield visor. I reached for it and noticed the return address was from the young woman he had been serious about back when he was in college. I asked permission to open it and read it.

With his consent I began to read how this young woman still had feelings for Steve and was hoping they could work out their relationship. My heart skipped a beat when I learned he had recently visited her. I was thinking, *Oh no. Oh no! I don't want him to start pursuing this girl again. If I don't say something to him now…I may never get another chance.*

When I decided to speak up, I didn't have the courage to look at him for fear of how he might respond. I took a deep breath and said, "I don't want you to pursue this girl."

"You don't? Why not?"

My heart pounded as I willed the words to come out of my mouth. "Because I always hoped one day you and I would end up together."

We sat in silence for what seemed like an eternity. Finally I mustered up the courage to look at Steve to try to read his expression. When our eyes met, a smile slowly came across his face as he replied, "Yeah. Me too."

"You too?"

Steve laughed as I threw my arms around his neck and gave him the biggest hug of his life!

## FIGURING IT OUT

Steve and I dated until I finished high school. While I wanted to get married right away, he wanted me to go to college and take some time to make sure marrying him was what I really wanted.

Steve knew learning to live on my own would be valuable to my maturity and a good experience to prepare me should we one day get married. Even while disappointed by Steve's plan, I recognized the wisdom in his suggestion. I moved out of my parents' home and into an apartment while working and attending a local college.

During that season of living on my own, I eventually landed a job in San Francisco, where each morning I took the 5:30 commuter train into the city. I loved the excitement of the job in the big city and the affirmation of my employers, who assured me they were going to help me build a career with great opportunities and travel.

All the while my heart was torn. My pride enjoyed the accolades from my bosses and drove me toward finding fulfillment in a successful career, but the other part of my heart realized how my walk with the Lord had suffered because of how busy I had become with work priorities. And since I was working from early morning until late evening, I saw Steve only on Saturdays—and even then I was so tired that our time together was less than satisfying for either of us.

Eventually Steve and I broke up, which crushed my heart in ways I never could have imagined. I tried focusing on all the opportunities my career would provide, yet a still, small voice often whispered, *This is not who you are. This is not what I created you for.*

Finally I could no longer deal with the struggle. I walked into my boss's office and said, "I need to resign."

He was shocked. "I don't understand. Why would you do that? You're going places. The company is going places. You're going to regret it."

But as the words had left my lips, my heart was relieved with my decision. I knew then and there the right thing to do was to quit the job and reassess my priorities. On the hour-long train ride home, I pondered what I had done. The more I considered, the more I was convinced the Lord was pleased with my decision.

## TOGETHER AGAIN

Learning of my decision, Steve asked if he could take me to dinner. I was elated. During our break up I had missed him terribly. And over dinner he told me how much he had missed me. By the time we finished dessert, we had agreed to give our relationship another go.

One day after a fun season of dating, Steve asked me to go with him to the mall. Knowing he hates the mall, I was surprised. But I agreed to go. I was so crazy in love with him, I would have gone anywhere with the man. (Come to think of it, 35 years later I'm even more crazy about him, and I'd still follow him anywhere.)

Steve led me by the hand into a jewelry store. I thought, *Oh, I wonder if he wants me to point out the kind of ring I like in case he ever wants to buy me an engagement ring.*

When the man behind the counter walked up and shook Steve's hand, I was surprised they knew one another. As Steve explained how the gentleman was an old family friend, the man disappeared into the back of the store. When he returned he handed Steve a small brown jewelry box. It was nearing my birthday, so I thought, *Maybe that's a gift for my birthday. Maybe the diamond earrings I've been wanting?*

To my surprise, Steve opened the box and pulled out an engagement ring. Right there in the middle of the jewelry store, he asked me to be his bride. I could hardly believe it! Steve and I had often talked about marriage, but the timing of his proposal took me completely by surprise.

I exclaimed "Yes!" as I threw my arms around his neck, crying and kissing his cheeks profusely.

When Steve assured me he had already obtained my father's permission to ask me to marry him, I immediately went into wedding-planning mode. Steve began looking for a house we could rent. The San Francisco Bay area housing was terribly expensive, so Steve and I never dreamed we would be able to afford to purchase a home. But one day we found a tiny 800-square-foot fixer upper (a dump, really) we could afford. Steve bought the house and immediately started remodeling it. For six months he worked until the house was an adorable little one-bedroom cottage ready for us to begin our lives together as husband and wife.

This remodeling experience ignited our passion to buy houses we could transform and sell for a profit. Because rent was so high in the Bay Area, we lived in the houses we were remodeling. That brought about all kinds of interesting ways for Steve and me to learn to sacrifice and work together toward a common goal. Our friends were in awe of how Steve could transform rundown houses into gorgeous homes. As soon as one house was completed, we sold it to buy yet another fixer upper. I always say back then people thought we were crazy. These days we would have a reality show!

## STEVE'S DREAM

While we were living in remodels, Steve also worked full-time in construction and we both volunteered in our church's youth ministry.

Steve's dream had always been to own property and be debt-free so we could serve the Lord wherever He might lead us. With each house we bought and sold, we were steps closer to living that dream.

I remember praying for many years, *Lord, please give us an opportunity to serve You in full-time ministry.*

After a season of Steve volunteering as interim youth pastor at our church, he came home from a meeting with our pastor and announced that he had been offered the full-time position as youth pastor. I was elated. I said, "Babe, this is what we've been praying for! You can finally work in full-time ministry and not be distracted by other jobs."

My heart sank when Steve responded, "I know. But I had to turn down the offer."

"What? Why?"

"Babe, we can't take that job. There is no way we could afford to live on the salary they offered."

With that realization Steve and I were broken before the Lord. We had been asking Him to use us, yet our finances made it difficult to respond to His call. We decided then and there to make some drastic changes.

## LIFE IN THE CANYON

One day Steve came home excited about a piece of property he'd found in the mountains. He said it was priced so we could afford it if we sold the house we were currently living in. It was snowing when we took the hour-and-a-half drive up a canyon to see the property. Our car struggled along the icy road until we met up with the Realtor, who drove us in his four-wheel-drive vehicle to see the house.

As we pulled up the dirt road, we saw an adorable little cottage covered with snow. I could see the look in Steve's eyes. This was the answer to his dream to own land and be debt-free. I'm not gonna lie. The idea scared me to death! The ranch was an hour up a winding road from the nearest town. And this city girl was not too keen on the idea of having a *Little House on the Prairie* experience. Our five-year-old daughter, however, was as elated as her daddy.

To make a long story short, after some serious prayer we signed on the dotted line, sold our house in the city, and moved up to the little cottage in the mountains. The day we moved in the snow had melted off the house, and the sweet little cottage looked to me more like a sad little shack.

Little did I realize it would take over two years to bring power to the house, and we lived with a generator all that time. Since we had to conserve power at night, we didn't watch as much television as we had in the past, which resulted in my getting pregnant with our third child. I'm laughing now, but you can bet I cried some tears when I realized I would be pregnant in such remote and challenging circumstances. Not to imply I didn't want another baby—I did. I just would never have planned to be pregnant until we had power, and Steve and I at least had our own bedroom.

Our two children slept in a bunk bed in the only bedroom while Steve and I slept on a sofa bed in the living room until Steve could finish adding on a master bedroom. I spent my entire pregnancy sleeping on the sofa bed. On many days Steve came home to a wife crying about the challenges of this new adventure we had taken together.

But in the end God granted us the dream He had put in my husband's heart to live in the country and to be debt-free. And Steve wisely added onto the house as we had the money, rather than taking out a mortgage against the house to do so.

Years later a small church down the backside of the canyon would call Steve to be their pastor. That's when we realized how being debt-free had been God's plan to prepare us to be able to accept a position in a little church that offered a small salary.

Our life in the canyon has brought many delightful adventures together as a family. Our children have since all grown up and moved away, but every chance they get they bring their families home to visit Gramma and Papa and all our farm animals at our big house in the country. And these days I realize how God has provided the perfect quiet place for me to spend time with Him, to study, and to write books.

As a young teen I met the love of my life. Even though at the time our age difference seemed so great, in God's timing He was preparing us not only to fall in love and live happily ever after, but for each of us to serve Christ in this generation—together. Life has certainly been an adventure for Steve and me, and we have no regrets. We agree we wouldn't go back to change one thing in our story (although Steve jokingly adds, "That's not true. I wouldn't have sold that Mach 1"). As we keep our eyes on Jesus, He continues to surprise us with the plans He has for us. And looking back we can truly celebrate that He has helped us build a "no-regrets marriage."

For more you can follow this link to listen to me tell the story: Cute Cottage or Shabby Shack? https://soundcloud.com/rhondastoppe/ chapter-8-cute-cottage-or-shack-stoppe

## PONDER THIS

Proverbs 16:9 reminds us, "A man's heart plans his way, but the LORD directs his steps." Looking back over my life, I realize this proverb has most certainly proven true as I recall God's faithfulness to guide me down the path He would have me follow.

To bring about a desired end result, we often contemplate and plan the way we should go. But God is the One who sees the beginning to the end. And He is the only one you can trust to work His perfect plan on your behalf—if you commit to walk in obedience to His ways.

Ponder Proverbs 20:24: "A man's steps are of the LORD; how then can a man understand his own way?"

*God is the only one you can trust to work His perfect plan on your behalf—if you commit to walk in obedience to His ways.*

Are you looking to God to guide your steps? It's easy to get distracted by relationships and career goals that will draw you away from the Lord's leading. But realizing that God's plan for you outweighs any way you might devise on your own should cause you to ponder if anything is holding back your passionate pursuit of Christ. How might

God be calling you to adjust your life so that you might discern His path for you?

If you're married, think back to when your love for your husband was new. Remember how your heart skipped a beat when he looked your way? I call those "magical moments." One of my favorite magical-moment memories is when my eyes locked onto Steve's when he was playing the alumni basketball game. It reminds me of how much I longed to have his attention and love, and pondering that feeling causes me to feel gratitude and contentment for Steve's love for me now.

*Working to remain content is a vital component to a happy marriage.*

Keeping the passion alive is another valuable step toward happiness in marriage. Look for ways to create new magical moments with your spouse.

Finally, recalling how much you ached to be loved by your husband and how happy you were when he returned your affection will help grow the love in your marriage. Reminding yourself of how much you longed to be loved by him is a great way to remain grateful for his affections. First Timothy 6:6 says, "Godliness with contentment is great gain." Working to remain content is a vital component to a happy marriage. Ask yourself if you work to live with an attitude of gratitude. If not, what changes can you make to grow a thankful heart toward your husband?

You can read more details of our love story and learn ways to create magical moments with your spouse in my book *The Marriage Mentor* (Harvest House Publishers, 2018). And follow our adventures in my social media posts: Facebook Page: Rhonda Stoppe No Regrets Woman, Instagram, & Twitter @RhondaStoppe. (I'd love to connect with you, so please take a moment to "like" my page and private message me a picture of you holding a copy of *Real-Life Romance*.)

2

*A Lifelong Love*

John and Denel

T he first time John and Denel met, she was 12 and John was a mature 14. They lived in the same neighborhood and had several mutual friends. John smiled as he recalled, "We didn't hang out at all, though. I just knew her as the cute lil' blonde who lived up the street."

That year, because of her dad's job transfer, Denel and her family moved to Michigan. Five years later her dad was transferred back to California. Then 17, Denel had kept in touch with her old friends, and she was thrilled to attend her senior year of high school with people familiar to her.

By that time John was no longer attending high school and was working at a steel mill. He laughed as he pointed out that he had not graduated from school, but because he had spun donuts on the school lawn he was granted an "early release"—his humorous way of saying he had been expelled.

John's best friend, Phillip, was in love with Denel. And since John was one of the few kids who had a job and drove a car, Phillip asked him to take him to where Denel worked. As they drove up to the drive-thru window, Phillip handed Denel a bouquet of flowers.

John was attracted to Denel immediately. Denel wished John was the guy bringing her the flowers.

## THAT CUTE LITTLE BLONDE

One day Phillip asked Denel to go with him to senior prom, and Denel was faced with a dilemma. She is one of those people who has a hard time saying no to anyone, but she knew she wanted to go to prom with John. She mustered up the courage to decline Phillip's invitation, giving him the "Can't we just be friends?" speech.

Denel was worried that John would never pursue her because he knew Phillip liked her. "You know, because of the whole best friend code guys have."

One day Denel saw John walking up their street, so she pulled over and offered him a ride home. John's truck was broken down, and he was happy to take the ride from "the cute little blonde."

John remembers, "She was driving her ugly, bright-yellow Pinto—a car I normally wouldn't have been caught dead in. But I was attracted to her, so I sucked up my pride and jumped into the car. I had kept my eye on Denel for some time, but I thought she would never be interested in me. She was definitely out of my league!"

As Denel pulled up to John's house, she decided it was time to show him how she felt. So before he got out of her car, Denel leaned over and kissed him. Then she asked him to be her date for her senior prom.

John agreed, and Denel was ecstatic. John's boss wouldn't give him the time off, though, so John surprised Denel and quit his job.

Denel knew then that John was the one she wanted to be with forever.

What Denel didn't know was that John quit, knowing his boss was swamped and desperate for workers, and that he'd be able to get his job back after prom.

Prom night was perfect, and from then on John and Denel were inseparable. John moved out on his own a year later, and he asked Denel to move in with him. Denel readily agreed. Neither was a Christian at the time, and they had no conviction against living together before marriage.

John and Denel had little money, and the neighborhood where they could afford to live was pretty rough. But the apartment manager took a liking to John and often allowed him to work around the complex in exchange for rent.

## ROMANCE IN A COFFEE CAN

On Christmas morning about a year after the two moved in together, John gave Denel a gift. When she opened it, she found a large can of coffee. Denel hates coffee and fought back tears of disappointment. She knew money was tight, but a can of coffee didn't seem like much of a Christmas gift.

As she held the coffee can, John jumped up to grab a can opener from the kitchen. He handed it to her and excitedly encouraged her to open the can.

Denel couldn't believe John wanted coffee right that minute, but she opened the can as John looked on. To her surprise, inside the can was a beautiful engagement ring. John got down on one knee and asked Denel to marry him, and she enthusiastically said yes!

Looking back, John and Denel can see God's sovereign hand in their story. Denel explained. "At the time John proposed, I was working for a mortgage company. Everyone who worked for the company was a Christian—everyone except me. I remember how strange it was to hear them say things like, 'Praise the Lord' and other stuff believers say to one another. But I also took notice of how kind they were to each other—and to me. It was something I had never been exposed to before, and it made an impression on me."

Before their wedding the chaplain asked Denel to choose a couple of scriptures for their ceremony. Denel had no idea how to comply with his request, so she asked a woman in her office for help.

The woman agreed and invited Denel to her house. Denel recalled, "The woman began to read to me from John chapter 15. When I heard how Jesus loved *me*, laid down His life for me, and wanted to abide in me, I cried. I had no idea why I was crying, but I couldn't stop."

The woman saw how the Holy Spirit was moving upon Denel's heart and asked her if she had ever received Christ. Denel had no idea what that meant, and she told her as much.

Then the woman walked Denel through scriptures that helped her realize how God loved her so much He sent His only Son to die to take away her sins and give her a new life in Christ (see John 3:16; Romans 6:11). Without hesitation, Denel prayed a prayer of repentance and invited Jesus to be her Lord and Savior.

Two weeks after Denel's conversion, she and John were married. John was 21 and Denel was 20.

Denel knew God had changed her heart, and she longed to grow in her faith. At work she joined in on Bible studies, but she was reluctant to attend church since John was not interested in such things.

Since they could afford to buy a home, the couple soon decided to move over an hour away from where they worked. Commuting together made Denel happy because it provided them with lots of time to talk. Also, she was relieved how their relocation removed her husband from the bad influence of his friends.

For three years Denel had been a Christian but had not involved herself in a church, knowing John would refuse to go. Denel continued to grow in her faith, however, through the influence of the godly women at work.

## A HOLE IN HER HEART

When Denel and John had their first child—a daughter named Cassie—they were completely devastated to learn she had a hole in her heart. Her condition was rare—and critical.

John and Denel took time off work to be at the hospital with their baby. With no income and medical bills mounting up, all they could do was hold their tiny daughter and wait to see if she would survive open-heart surgery.

Denel prayed like she had never prayed before, and God answered her prayer with successful surgery. Soon she and John took their fragile baby home to recover. You can imagine how frightened Denel was as she felt the weight of the responsibility of caring for Cassie. "For the surgery, they had to cut her chest completely open. For fear the incision would split open, I was afraid to even allow her to cry. I felt overwhelmed, alone, and exhausted. I knew it was time for me to find a church."

*With no income and medical bills mounting up, all they could do was hold their tiny daughter and wait to see if she would survive open-heart surgery.*

Denel told John, "I'm sorry if you don't want to go to church. I received Christ a few years ago, and I'm going whether you go or not—and I'm taking Cassie with me."

Although John knew he should agree to attend church with Denel, he didn't want to. Denel went to church alone.

After a few weeks, their next-door neighbor came over to see how John and Denel were getting along caring for Cassie and all her health issues. The neighbor had invited John to church several times, but this time when he did John agreed to give it a try. Denel was delighted to hear her husband consent to visit the church. And she was even more surprised when the very next Sunday John was up and ready to go to church with her.

For the first time, John experienced church not as a place where people performed rituals, but rather a place filled with people who seemed to love God—and one another.

After a year of listening to Pastor Phil preach from the Bible, one Sunday morning during the message John thought, *This is what God has for me.* With that, John quietly surrendered his heart to Christ.

Denel saw an immediate change in John once he gave his heart to Jesus. The two never looked back.

Over 25 years ago my husband and I met John and Denel at the very church where John surrendered his heart to Christ. Steve and I were instantly drawn to the couple because of their sweet love for one another.

As John and Denel told me the details of their love story, it was so cute to watch the two of them light up as they shared their sweet memories. They were finishing one another's sentences, laughing at their awkwardness, and correcting one another to get the chronological order of their story right. We all marveled at the Lord's hand of providence in their lives.

God caused John and Denel's paths to cross when they were children, and then He brought them back together when they were old enough to fall in love. Even though they didn't know anything about God's love for them, He loved them anyway. Even when they didn't walk according to His commands, He wooed them. And after God allowed their daughter to be born in critical condition, He used the situation to draw John to Christ.

Denel shared, "I am forever grateful that the Lord blessed me with John. Looking back, I realize our lives could have turned out so differently had God not brought us to Christ. God has treated us with undeserved mercy and grace. He has blessed us with two children who love Christ, and by His grace they are seeking to honor Him with their lives."

## PONDER THIS

God knew John and Denel would one day surrender their hearts to Christ. In His kindness, He brought the two of them together—even before they were Christians. The Lord led Denel to work with believers who showed her Christ's love and explained the gospel. Later God used their daughter's birth defect to draw John to a relationship with Jesus as well.

*God made a way for them to fall in love, and
ultimately to fall in love with Jesus so they could
serve Him together for the rest of their lives.*

Romans 5:8 says, "God demonstrates His own love toward us, in that while we were still sinners, Christ died for us." In keeping with His attribute of unconditional love, while John and Denel were yet sinners, God made a way for them to fall in love, and ultimately to fall in love with Jesus so they could serve Him together for the rest of their lives.

## ASK YOURSELF

Do you understand how sin separates you from God? Experiencing a true heart change requires that you realize you are a sinner and agree with God that the only way to be cleansed from your sins is to go to Him for forgiveness through Jesus's sacrifice on the cross. John 14:6 says, "Jesus said to him, 'I am the way, the truth, and the life. No one comes to the Father except through Me.'"

And once you turn to Jesus, He will guide you toward the life He had planned for you all along (see Ephesians 2:8-10).

To learn more please read in the appendix *How to Have a Relationship with Jesus.*

# 3
## *Waiting on God's Timing*

### Kevin and Suzanne

Suzanne tied the final knot on the fortieth "wordless book" beaded bracelet she'd made that evening in preparation for Vacation Bible School the next day. She slipped one of the bracelets over her wrist. She had worn the colorful bracelet many times since she was a teen, using it as a tool to teach children the message of the gospel. Sharing the gospel with kids and teaching them to love Jesus had always been one of her passions.

Normally, Suzanne would have gone right to bed after she finished her project. But she had promised to meet a friend for coffee, and she headed to her favorite coffee shop.

When Suzanne stepped up to the counter, the tall young man behind the counter grinned at her. "Where did you get that bracelet?" he asked.

The barista was genuinely interested, especially when she explained she had made 40 of them to hand out at Vacation Bible School. "I could do VBS every day for the rest of my life," she said.

The young man's grin widened. "I'm going to be a children's pastor! I've been doing children's ministry for ten years."

Suzanne was intrigued. *I've never met a man who wants to be a children's pastor,* she thought.

While the barista made her latte, Suzanne learned the young man's name was Kevin and that they attended the same church. It was a large church, so it was no surprise that the two had never met before. Suzanne left the coffee shop that night wondering if meeting Kevin was mere coincidence or if there could be more to their relationship. Over the next several weeks she saw Kevin a number of times at the coffee shop.

## HE'S TOO YOUNG

One day she stopped in for coffee with a coworker. When Suzanne pointed out Kevin to her friend, she said, "Oh, yeah! Kevin was part of our college ministry last year." Suzanne learned that Kevin had graduated from college only a month before they met. Suzanne was 30. Realizing their age difference, Suzanne mentally moved on from any romantic thoughts she may have been entertaining.

"In my decade of singleness since college, I'd become a pro at letting go easily," Suzanne said. "When I realized Kevin was much younger, it wasn't hard to cross him off the potential suitor list. I was disappointed because I could see he was special, but I accepted the fact that the age difference was too big and moved on."

Suzanne had grown up the oldest of four children and had always been mature for her age. Her mom used to tell her she would likely marry an older, more mature man. "You'll recognize the right guy when he shows up," her mom assured her. With her mother's voice in her head, leaving behind any idea of a relationship with Kevin seemed like a sensible decision.

As a high school student, Suzanne had never dated anyone. And through her college years, studies had kept her occupied. She just kind of assumed the right guy would show up after she graduated from college.

Upon graduation Suzanne moved to Colorado where she had landed a great job as a children's magazine editor for Focus on the Family. After a few years she became a regular contributor to Boundless—a website for Christian young adults.[1]

## TIRED OF BEING ALONE

Suzanne was content in her singleness—most days. Colorado offered a wonderful community for Christian singles and had several great churches where she could connect and serve. However, by her late twenties Suzanne experienced what many single adult women go through. "I had begun to tire of being on my own. I watched many of my friends marry and start their families. And while I believed I was walking obediently with the Lord and that I could trust Him with my future, I sometimes felt forgotten."

During the loneliest times Suzanne clung to the promises in the Bible that God would direct her steps, just as He had directed the steps of those He led in the pages of Scripture. She would often find strength in reminding herself that Christ was her ultimate hope, joy, and purpose.

Suzanne had been taught to view Christian marriage and courtship as a race. "I had been running that race alone throughout my twenties. Sometimes I would look over and catch a glimpse of someone, but inevitably they would veer off in another direction or pass me by. Even a few godly relationships just did not click. In those moments, I would cry out to the Lord and try to understand His love and His purpose for me."

*During the loneliest times Suzanne clung to the*
*promises in the Bible that God would direct her steps.*

One of Suzanne's lowest points came one New Year's Day. She recounted, "New Year's Day was one of my loneliest ever. I ended the day in a sniveling heap on my bed, shedding tears on my Bible and listening to worship music. The only insight I could come up with was that God knows and He loves."

Rather than allowing herself to become discouraged, Suzanne determined to focus on living life in a way that honored God—while trying her hand at a multitude of new activities. She found that she enjoyed improv comedy, running, and coffee tastings. However, a longing in her heart to one day enjoy these things with a husband remained.

Suzanne saw Kevin from time to time at church because he had been hired as an elementary children's ministry coordinator. "I would say hi when I passed him in the halls on Sunday, but any thought of him as a romantic possibility was gone," Suzanne remembers. "I thought my connection with the handsome barista was just a fluke."

## THERE HE IS AGAIN

In the fall of that year, Suzanne organized an improv comedy show as a church fundraiser. Kevin signed up to perform. Suzanne enjoyed Kevin's talent and charisma, but she refused to entertain any romantic feelings toward him. She observed Kevin's character and came to admire his kindness and willingness to serve others.

One day when Suzanne dropped her car off at the local auto shop, one of the employees who knew she served in children's ministry told her he had begun to pray for the sixth graders she was teaching—*and* he was praying for God to send Suzanne a husband who shared the same heart for children's ministry.

"Kevin popped into my mind," Suzanne said. "Kevin was one of the only single guys I knew doing children's ministry…the thought lingered. Until that shuttle driver's prayer, I had not considered it important or necessary to marry someone who shared my heart for children. Still, the nudge was not strong enough to overcome what I saw as an insurmountable barrier in our age difference."

## SOMETHING SPECIAL

About four months after Suzanne's conversation with the man in the auto shop, she received an email from Kevin inviting her to co-lead a young adult Bible study with him. Suzanne agreed to meet with Kevin to discuss his request. That night they ended up talking for several hours, at the same coffee shop where they first met. Soon they were seeing each other weekly at their small group study and planning meetings.

"Within weeks of starting the group, we each knew we had found something special in the other," Suzanne said. "I responded to Kevin's leadership, enthusiasm, and desire for God, and he responded to my encouragement, strength, and heart for ministry."

The age difference that had been a barrier in Suzanne's mind was no longer an issue. When Kevin initiated the relationship, Suzanne was encouraged by people who served in ministry with them. The church rejoiced because they could see the work God was doing to bring together these two servants.

It wasn't long before Kevin asked Suzanne to be his wife. After a six-month engagement, they married. Eight years later, they have four lively children. They continue to serve together in children's and family ministry.

Looking back, Suzanne realizes how God caused their paths to cross. She is confident of God's provision and guidance in their lives, and she likes to say God is the best matchmaker.

When Kevin and Suzanne were single, God placed each one where He wanted them to serve Him. Both were running the race God had set before them. With eyes fixed on Jesus, they continued to do the ministry He put in their hearts, and in His perfect timing God used a wordless book bracelet to initiate a love that would last a lifetime.[2]

## PONDER THIS

In Jeremiah 29:11 God says, "I know the plans I have for you... plans to prosper you and not to harm you, plans to give you hope and a future" (NIV). If you're single, how might this verse encourage your heart? Think of it, the creator of heaven and earth knows you—you! And He knows how much you long to be married.

Learning to trust God's character can sometimes be challenging when the longing of your heart isn't satisfied. But love stories like Kevin and Suzanne's offer hope and inspiration. Be encouraged by Suzanne's statement: "God knows and He loves."

## ASK YOURSELF

Do you ever feel forgotten by God? If you're single, can you choose to trust God with your future? Like Suzanne, will you determine to take your eyes off your disappointment and devote yourself to loving Christ and serving Him? And then trust Him for the outcome?

Many women I meet hope God will bring them a godly man, but they themselves do not pursue a godly life. You are mistaken if you think God will bring you a man who is passionately pursuing the Lord if you aren't living righteously. How might you adjust your life to take your focus off looking for a husband and learn to find contentment in loving and serving Jesus?

# 4
## The Heart's True Desire

Jason and Noelle

Imagine the cutest little town, one with a palm tree-lined main street, apricot orchards on every corner, and incredible pink skies each evening as the sun set behind the mountain range across the glorious farmlands to the west. Church bells chimed at the top of each hour and could be heard by the students who attended the only high school in town.

This is where Jason and Noelle grew up.

The kids in that small town had a unique bond that can be found only in such a quaint community. As in most agricultural towns, a festival celebrated their harvest—in this case, apricots. One year Noelle even entered the town's Apricot Fiesta pageant and was named first runner-up.

Noelle had an identical twin sister named Nicole. The girls had fun confusing their friends and teachers as to who was who. Noelle remembers how much fun they had tricking Jason from time to time. "When you fall in love with a twin, you get a package deal. We all hung out together and had lots of fun."

Life seemed to be perfect. And it only made sense that Jason and 16-year-old Noelle would begin to date. Noelle recalled, "We both loved sports, and we were extremely competitive. Whenever I was looking for a mate for tennis, softball, even knee boarding, I found myself hoping Jason would be my teammate. It was always just way more fun when I was with Jason."

Noelle couldn't have asked for a better boyfriend. "Jason spoiled me. He would tell me he loved me and that I was beautiful more than any girl needs to be told."

Jason was one of the good guys too. He wasn't involved in partying, and he was extremely loyal and trustworthy. "Jason protected my purity too. Even though it wasn't his conviction to wait for marriage, he honored my conviction and never pressured me. I was convinced Jason was a keeper."

After three years of dating Jason, Noelle's life was changed forever when she began to attend a college-age Bible study group in her small town.

"Through the teaching of the Word, the Lord made Himself known to me. I realized that my life up to that point had been all about me and what I could get out of it. When I learned God sent His Son so I could have new life in Christ, the Holy Spirit made the gospel irresistible to me and I surrendered my heart to Jesus as my Lord and Savior."

The more Noelle grew in her faith, the more God convicted her about her relationship with Jason. "As I learned how God wanted me to lay down anything I loved more than Him, I became extremely convicted because I knew my relationship with Jason was something I idolized."

Jason was not a Christian, and Noelle knew God would not want her to marry a man who wasn't a believer. At first Noelle was tempted to think if she could just get Jason to become a Christian, then they could continue dating. But she knew that was the wrong motivation for wanting Jason to know Christ.

Noelle sincerely loved Jason, and she longed for him to know the same new life in Jesus she experienced. She began to invite Jason to the Bible study and to attend church with her. Often she would tell him how much she wanted him to find forgiveness in Jesus.

At one point Jason professed to have been saved. After about a year, however, Noelle realized Jason's life reflected no genuine heart change. Noelle remembers, "He was still a really great guy, but the motivations of his heart hadn't changed. Where he looked to find his worth hadn't changed. He didn't display any evidence of a person walking intimately with the Lord."

## THE SURRENDER

With this realization, the Spirit began to convict Noelle that she needed to surrender her relationship with Jason to the Lord. Noelle was in love with Jason, and she wanted to spend the rest of her life with him. But she had no peace about the prospect of marriage to a man who didn't share her same love for Christ. Faced with the enormity of the decision, Noelle wrestled with her thoughts. *Do I really trust that God's way is best?*

A moment of clarity came to Noelle when God brought to her mind Romans 8:18: "I consider that the sufferings of this present time are not worth comparing to the glory that will be revealed in us" (NIV).

With an ache in her heart, Noelle resolved she would end her relationship with Jason. Tearfully, she tried to explain to him her reasons for the break up. In his usual kind manner, Jason responded that he wanted for Noelle only what would make her happy.

*Do I really trust that God's way is best?*

Many nights Noelle cried herself to sleep. She often reached for the phone to call Jason, but then she would remind herself to obey the conviction the Lord had placed on her heart.

As she grieved, she prayed. Noelle described the dichotomy of emotions she felt. "I was miserable in my flesh, but happy in Christ. The more I focused on Jesus and His love for me, meditated on Scripture, and prayed for strength, the more at peace I became over the break up."

Noelle was glad Jason continued to attend Bible study and church, but it also made social gatherings awkward and painful. They were cordial to each other, but they were careful not to be alone together. Gradually Noelle and Jason felt they were "getting over each other."

*The more I focused on Jesus and His love for me,
meditated on Scripture, and prayed for strength, the
more at peace I became over the break up.*

As Jason continued to fellowship with other believers and listen to the teaching of God's Word, the Spirit graciously brought him to genuine repentance. One day the Lord opened his mind to understand that the words he had said in the past to "receive Christ" were just that—words, and without any real commitment. Quietly, Jason prayed for God to forgive him of his sins and asked Him to be the Lord of his life.

Jason didn't share with Noelle that he had truly been saved. But Noelle remembered how differently Jason began to act. "His motivation was different; *he* was different."

However, Noelle had not broken up with Jason only because he wasn't a Christian. She also had been convicted that she was putting him first over her relationship with Christ. By now Noelle's focus was on loving Jesus, and she didn't want to become distracted by her old flame for Jason. She continued to take her thoughts captive and seek the Lord.

By that time her twin sister had also surrendered to Christ, along with a few of their other girlfriends, and Noelle enjoyed sweet fellowship with her sisters in Christ. Noelle was content to think she was completely over Jason.

After almost a year, Noelle was taken aback when their college leader pulled her aside. "You know, you should take a look at Jason. He's a completely different person now. Spend some time in prayer about him. I know at one time you both really cared for each other and enjoyed each other's company. You are both believers and of the same mind now, and you're moving in the same direction. Pray about it."

Noelle didn't know how to process the possibility of having Jason back in her life. By now she was convinced he wouldn't even want a relationship with her. She also had to evaluate her own insecurity and pride.

"Jason had clearly moved on. He was totally over me. What was I going to do or say? 'Uh, sorry I dumped you. But you're an amazing man of God now and I want you back—please!' Because of my pride,

I couldn't imagine those words coming out of my mouth. For the next week I went back and forth between praying for the Lord's will and struggling with my humility."

While she waited for God's answer, Noelle completely avoided Jason. She spent hours a day in prayer and reading the Bible, and she tried to talk herself out of having feelings for him again.

Then one day she came across Psalm 37:4: "Delight yourself also in the LORD, and He shall give you the desires of your heart."

Noelle remembered how she had been taught that the true meaning of Psalm 37:4 did *not* mean, "If you're happy in God, He will give you whatever you want."

Noelle told me, "As I pondered the truth about God's ways, it dawned on me. If I am delighting in Him, His desires will become my desires."

When Noelle came to understand that while she was making her priority to know and love Christ, He in turn was making her heart and motives Christ-focused rather than self-focused.

"At that point, what drew me to desire a relationship with Jason was not the same motivation as before. Daily I was becoming more enthralled to watch God's transforming power in Jason's life. And it caused me to give honor and glory to the Lord. Not only was the life change in him something that made me want to be around him, but his heart and love for others made me love him even more. He had become a servant of the Lord whose priorities had changed. Jason now valued drawing near to the Lord and serving Him as the most valuable way to spend his life. When I considered Jason's heart to know God and his love for others, I couldn't help but love Jason all the more."

Finally Noelle realized God would honor her desire to fall in love with Jason again. But what would Jason think? Noelle was fearful that he might not return her affections.

"After days of gut-wrenching procrastination, I seized the opportunity to be alone with Jason, and I humbly shared with him all that was going on in my heart and mind."

To Noelle's disappointment, Jason didn't react with the enthusiasm she had hoped for. After a long silence, he responded. "This is really catching me off guard. I hadn't even considered that you and I would ever be together again."

Noelle's heart sank.

But then Jason said, "I need to spend some time alone with the Lord and seek His will in this. And I really think I should seek out some godly counsel as well."

Noelle remembers thinking, *Jason's mature response makes me love him even more.*

As Noelle waited for Jason to come to a decision, she prayed for God to grant him discernment to know His will.

It wasn't long before Jason showed up on Noelle's doorstep with a big smile on his face. Noelle knew just from looking at Jason that God had put in his heart the same answer He'd put in her heart.

As Jason embraced Noelle, he professed his deep love for her. He then took time to make sure Noelle understood how they would need to commit their relationship to the Lord. They agreed that their love for Christ would always take priority over their love for each other.

Jason and Noelle began their relationship anew. Built on loving and serving God, they learned how deeply they could love each other when Christ was the center of their love.

After a year of building their relationship on the love of Christ, Jason was confident Noelle was the one he wanted by his side for the rest of his life. Six months later they were married.

Over the next several years, God gave Jason and Noelle two beautiful daughters, and the Lord graced them with a beautiful little boy adopted from Ethiopia.

Jason and Noelle smile when they remember how God graciously transformed the priorities of two athletic high schoolers who believed they were content to live out their small-town lives enjoying all the things they thought were important.

Jason and Noelle have now been married for more than a decade, and they still can't believe how God brought them back together. These days you can find them playing softball for the small-town league, playing dodgeball with a bunch of teens, and coaching their kids' sporting events. But now the focus of their activities is to let the love of Christ shine brightly as they love each other with Christ's self-less love.

Jason and Noelle's love was initially a self-focused love because they looked to each other to fill the void only God can truly satisfy. Once they each came to know Christ, God led them to realize how they had individually made their relationship an idol. God graciously did a work in their hearts so that loving Christ became their priority.

If God desires that with all our being we put no other relationship above loving Him (Mark 12:30), how would you say you're measuring up to His desire for your marriage (or dating) relationship?

If you're single, are you willing to trust God for His best for your future? Ask Him to show you if your relationship is self-focused or Christ-centered. Are you willing to submit your future to God's desire and wait on Him to bring a spouse who will help you love and serve God for the rest of your life?

# 5

# The Way Christ Forgives

### Nate and Jillian

When you're in ministry long enough, you get the privilege of watching several young couples fall in love. Jillian and Nate were just such a couple. Steve and I knew Nate as an awesome young man who worked at a camp where Steve and I often spoke.

Years ago I was so impressed with the godly character qualities Nate displayed that I interviewed him for my book *Moms Raising Sons to Be Men*. I wanted to find out how his mother influenced the man he had become. When I asked Nate to describe his mother in one word, without hesitation he said, "*Forgiving.* My mother is the most forgiving person I know."

Jillian was raised in a wonderful Christian home. She grew up in the church, and she was the little sister of our worship pastor. I got a firsthand look at how God brought Nate and Jillian together. I clearly remember seeing their budding romance the night of my youngest daughter's wedding. The two of them stood outside the reception hall chatting and laughing, and I had one of those "Oh yes. This would be a wonderful couple" matchmaker moments!

## "I GOT BUTTERFLIES"

Jillian had seen Nate several times at the camp where he worked and remembers being attracted to his tall-dark-and-handsome features. He was the guy who always got into character for dress-up nights. Whether he was decked out in full cowboy attire or dressed as a ninja or a Jedi, Nate most certainly stood out to Jillian as she watched him from afar.

Jillian playfully recalled feeling a bit of unexpected jealousy when one day she saw Nate walking close to a girl. She secretly wished *she* was the girl with whom he was walking, though she had never once spoke to Nate.

Jillian decided she needed to make herself known to Nate. "The next time I saw him, I *actually* talked to him and I gave him some sassy attitude, so he would remember me."

Several months passed before Nate and Jillian officially met again. He came to town to meet up with Jillian's older brother and some other friends they both had in common.

Jillian walked right over to Nate and said, "Hi, Nate. I'm Nathan's sister—Jillian." To which Nate responded, "I know." (In case you're confused, let me be clear that Jillian's brother's name is Nathan as well.)

Jillian had no idea their friends had invited Nate to come to the event so he could meet her. Nate, on the other hand, thought Jillian was in on the plan when he playfully responded to her introduction. Jillian, however, considered his awkward response "super rude," and they didn't talk the rest of the night. (Don't you just hate when two people meet and you know they would make an amazing couple but they can't get past the awkward intros?)

A few days later Jillian received a friend request from Nate on social media. She recalls, "I stared at it for a while, thinking, *He didn't talk to me. Why would he want to be my friend?* But I thought he was really cute, and I knew we had a lot of friends in common, so I added him."

Nathan later shared with Jillian that he sent the friend request so he could see if she had a boyfriend. And he jokingly admits he stalked her profile for a while before getting up enough courage to message her.

"I will never forget the very first message he sent to me," Jillian said. "I immediately got butterflies. It had been a few days since I had seen him, but for some reason I was still thinking about him."

Nate's message read, "After some late night social media stalking, I decided we should be *real* friends and not just online friends."

Jillian messaged back, and from that day on messaging became their number one way of communicating. The camp where Nate worked was in the mountains, so he had poor cell phone service.

Jillian remembers what that was like. "Every morning I would check my messages to see if I had one from him, and I got excited every time I did. Nate would tell me about what he was reading in the Bible. Or sometimes we would read through a passage together and talk about how it applied to our lives. I had never talked with a guy like that before. The guys I had known talked about how pretty I was and flattered me for all the wrong reasons. Nate talked to me like a friend—a sister in Christ."

Over the next several months, Nate and Jillian spent time together in the company of friends. They went ice skating at an outdoor ice rink in the mountains near Nate's home—how romantic! And then Nate would make the two-hour drive down to where Jillian lived to join her and their friends on outings. Their trip to the Monterey Bay Aquarium is one of Jillian's favorite memories.

One day Nate invited Jillian—and several friends—to join him on a trip to visit his parents at a different camp where they lived and worked. Jillian remembers how excited she was about the trip, and then how freaked out she became when all their friends bailed on the trip except Nate and her.

> Nate promised himself: "I will not tell another
> girl I love you unless it can be forever."

Jillian recalled, "The few hours of driving to meet his parents were really sweaty for me. I was so nervous. Here is this guy who loves the Lord *and* who gives me butterflies. I never thought I would deserve a guy like him because my dating record was not the best."

Nate noticed the awkward silence in the car, so he broke the ice. "I like you. But I want to keep our friendship the way it is because dating just adds physical pressure that isn't necessary. I promised myself I will not tell another girl *I love you* unless it can be forever."

Nate then made a statement that took Jillian's breath away. "The next girlfriend I have will be my wife. I don't even want to kiss another girl until I know she will be my wife."

In reaction to what Nate had just said, it was all Jillian could do not to let her jaw drop open. She composed herself and told Nate she agreed that their relationship should remain the same. But inwardly she was thinking, *How can this guy really like me? Me!*

That evening Jillian enjoyed meeting Nate's family. And the next day Nate took Jillian on a lovely hike. All the while, Jillian carried a huge weight in her heart. She thought to herself, *If this guy really likes me, he needs to know I haven't been a great example of a Christian.*

With every ounce of courage Jillian could muster, she stopped dead in her tracks and revealed to Nate her darkest secret. "Nate, I am not a virgin."

With her eyes fixed on the path in front of her because she couldn't bear to look into Nate's kind eyes, she went on. "I chose to not listen to God's Word, even though I had been taught that what He tells us to avoid is for our own good."

Jillian held her breath awaiting Nate's response. She thought, *Here is this godly guy who doesn't want to even kiss a woman until they are engaged to be married. What is he gonna say?*

When she raised her eyes, Nate looked deep into them and asked, "Have you repented? Did you ask God to forgive you?"

Jillian humbly replied, "Yes. Yes I have."

Nate simply responded, "Then I forgive you too." And he continued walking down the path.

Nate's words were too good to be true! "In that moment I knew Nate was the man I was going to marry. Nate has never asked for details. He has never brought it up again. He simply forgave me the way Christ forgives."

Several months went by as Nate and Jillian continued to be "friends who knew they liked each other," as they put it. In June their relationship got serious when Nate asked Jillian's father if he could date her. Jillian knew this meant Nate was looking toward one day asking her to be his wife.

Then in October Nate got down on one knee and said, "Jillian Irene, I love you. Will you be my wife?"

That's when Jillian kissed him for the very first time! "I couldn't wait any longer!" she told me.

After they kissed, Nate gave her a strange look. She had forgotten to say yes. Jillian said, "I was so excited to be *that* girl that he would walk close to for the rest of our lives. And I would get to be the one who would *always* be his girlfriend."

Nate explained to Jillian that, when they visited his parents, he told them "she's the one." He had even shown them the ring he had already purchased for her. She was blessed to learn that Nate's parents had been praying for her by name from the first day they met her.

## THE ENGAGEMENT

Jillian said this about the engagement:

> We had only a five-month engagement—I do not know how people stay pure for any longer! I wanted to be his wife so badly. We had set such great purity lines for our friendship and dating, but once kissing started, man, was that a difficult boundary to keep.
>
> The two-hour distance was great for building our relationship through communication. And then when we were visiting each other, we tried to keep a group of friends around while we talked wedding details.
>
> We did premarital counseling with Steve and Rhonda Stoppe—for six *long* weeks. I say long because Nate was driving two hours every session (just one way!), and I always cried after he left.
>
> I am so glad we made the effort to seek out premarital counseling. What we learned was so valuable.
>
> *Saving sex for our wedding night gave us a bond that is deeper than just physical attraction.*
>
> Waiting until marriage to do anything but kiss really built our trust. Nate loved me enough to wait—even though the

world we live in accepts so much more than that. Some of my non-Christian friends questioned why we were waiting and tried to convince me our sex life after marriage would struggle if we didn't know we were "compatible" before we married. Or they cautioned me that I might be stuck with a husband who didn't satisfy me. Boy, were they wrong!

Looking back, I can see how saving sex for our wedding night gave us a bond that is deeper than just physical attraction. We have learned that God really does know what's best. He did design marriage, after all!

## PONDER THIS

God forgives to the utmost. So much so that He forgave Jillian of all her past sins and faithfully drew her and Nate together to fall in love, showing the reality of Christ's complete forgiveness in the way Nate responded to Jillian when she shared her secret. His immediate response was to forgive Jillian as Christ had forgiven her.

How might Nate's mother's example of being a forgiving person prepared him to forgive Jillian without condition?

## ASK YOURSELF

What stood out to you most in Nate and Jillian's story? If you're single, maybe you find yourself in a situation similar to Jillian's—regretting some sinful past choices. Have you gone to the Lord and asked His forgiveness? Are you willing to turn from any relationship based on sex rather than on honoring Christ with sexual purity?

When God cleanses you from sin, He promises complete forgiveness. Psalm 51:7 says, "Purge me with hyssop, and I shall be clean; wash me, and I shall be whiter than snow."

What hope God offers to anyone who turns from sin to walk in obedience to His will and His ways. Jillian's story reveals God's kindness in bringing her to repentance and then guiding her to a godly man who would forgive her and love her for the rest of her life.

# 6

## A Kiss Will Only Complicate Things

### James and Missy

Missy grew up dreaming of "the one" who would sweep her off her feet. Her parents had married right out of high school, and she dreamed of living the same life her parents had enjoyed together. Missy admired her mother and hoped to be just like her.

Since Missy's mom had never gone to college, Missy decided not to go either. When she met a young widow with two small children, however, she considered what would happen to her if she one day found herself in a similar situation. Missy finally decided to go to college after high school when her grandmother said, "You never know what can happen in life. Having a college degree can give you something to fall back on."

College was better than Missy had imagined. She liked school so much she went on to earn her master's degree and become a physical therapist. She dated a bit, but she quickly grew weary of the shallowness of the dating life. Although Missy's relationships with men were disappointing, her relationship with the Lord was flourishing as she enjoyed alone time with Him.

While waiting to catch a plane one day after graduating, she watched several pilots pass by. Missy surprised herself when she turned to her friend and said, "I want to marry a pilot." The more she pondered the idea, the more she thought marrying a pilot would be a dream come true.

The very next month a new patient walked into Missy's life. James was handsome and charming. After sharing a professional conversation, he asked Missy if he might have her business card. "As a professional contact," he said.

When Missy gave him her card, she never considered any hope of romance to come of their meeting.

For the next two weeks, James couldn't get Missy off his mind. He was smitten with her from the start. When he finally got up the nerve to call her, he hinted that he wanted to ask her out on a date. By this time Missy had so dismissed her first meeting with James that she was having a hard time remembering who he was. She explained he was a stranger and she needed to be cautious. Missy said, "I am in no hurry to date some guy I just met."

James respected her resolve to be cautious. He admired that she wasn't an easy catch.

To Missy's delight, James suggested they get to know each other over the phone. Every night the two talked for hours. Missy was intrigued when James told her he was a pilot. She also admired his intelligence, his charm, and his funny, easygoing manner. The way James made Missy feel as though he was genuinely interested in what she had to say made her like him even more.

Despite Missy's growing affection for James, one thing was standing in the way of her wanting a relationship with him. James was not a Christian.

Missy knew she would never marry someone who was not a believer. Her love for the Lord was the most important thing in her life. Being married to someone who couldn't share that passion was simply out of the question.

> *Despite Missy's growing affection for James, one thing was standing in the way of her wanting a relationship with him. James was not a Christian.*

When Missy finally agreed to go out with James, they met at a casual restaurant. Over dinner Missy couldn't help but enjoy James's charming personality. For their second date, she invited James to a drama production her church was hosting. The play portrayed an after-death depiction of the consequence of rejecting Christ.

Missy said, "What a second date, right? The poor guy didn't know what he was in for when I invited him to that play!"

After the show James and Missy went out for pizza and had a serious talk about her faith. Then James looked into Missy's eyes and inquired, "What exactly are you looking for in a relationship?"

She took a deep breath and honestly explained. "I want to marry a man who's a Christian and lives to serve Christ. I need a husband who will be the spiritual leader of our family. And I'll settle for nothing less."

Missy could see the disappointment in James's eyes. She wondered if he could read hers as well when he responded, "Then I guess that's the end of our spending time together, huh?"

Missy forced herself to respond. "Yeah, I guess so."

As James walked Missy to her car, both were deeply saddened when it came time to say good-bye. They had grown to care for each other and parting was not going to be easy.

Missy remembers, "When James asked if he could kiss me good-bye, my heart dropped because I had to say no."

She could see the sense of rejection in James's face when he asked her why he couldn't give her a simple kiss good-bye. She knew her feelings for James were deeper than she should have allowed them to be. She answered, "Because kissing you will only complicate things."

James's response took Missy by surprise. "Your strength impresses me. We obviously like each other, and you are willing to let that all go because of your faith and relationship with God. There must be something real about all of that. I would like to know more."

Missy could hardly believe it when James continued, "Would it be all right if I started going to church with you?"

Missy laughed and said, "Yes—but we are not dating!"

## FIREWORKS

To Missy's delight James met her weekly at the young adult group at her church, where they listened to sound teaching and enjoyed outings with the group. "We were able to spend lots of time together without actually dating," she said.

After six months of James attending church, Missy watched in joyful amazement as one Sunday he walked the aisle to surrender his life to Jesus.

Although Missy was elated, she was also cautious. She wanted to be sure James's commitment to Christ was genuine and not just something he did so she would date him.

Missy prayed for God's wisdom as she observed James's new life in Christ. What she saw confirmed to her that his salvation was genuine, and she knew she could finally allow her heart to fall hopelessly in love with James.

Missy remembers, "I fell in love with James at a party for my work. James was so full of fun and life. When he pulled me close and our eyes locked, I saw fireworks in our eyes."

From then on James and Missy were inseparable. "We were dating for real," Missy told me, laughing.

On the ten-month anniversary of the day they met, James took Missy out to celebrate. She'd known something was up when James told her to dress fancy. When they arrived at a nice restaurant, the hostess, quite excitedly, welcomed them and walked them to a private booth. On the table was a bouquet of ten red roses, "One for each month of our time together," James told her.

Over dinner the two laughed as they shared memories of how the Lord had brought them together. If ever a girl was "hard to get," it was Missy. But James got her and he never wanted to let her go.

After dinner James got down on one knee as he pulled out a little jewelry box. He hardly finished asking Missy to marry him when she joyfully responded, "Yes!"

## NO BABY BLUES

Six months later, James and Missy were married. After a romantic honeymoon in Hawaii, they settled into married life. Missy recalled, "Our first year was good, but definitely an adjustment period! I was 27 and James was 29. We had both lived on our own for quite a while. We had to learn to be 'we' instead of 'me!'"

Over the next several years, the couple enjoyed marriage as they learned to live in unity. Although their union was blissful, they wrestled with disappointment when month after month Missy was unable to get pregnant.

After three years of praying and doctor appointments, God blessed them with a baby girl they named Jayleen. To signify how truly united the couple had become, they chose that name as a combination of their middle names.

Missy was finally able to realize her dream to be a stay-at-home wife and mother. But because James was working as a private pilot for minimal pay and no health coverage, quitting her job brought financial challenges. Yet God provided in a miraculous way. Just two weeks after Jayleen was born, they were guaranteed a better income and health care when James got accepted into flight school with the National Guard. It was a dream come true for him.

After James's two-year training with the Guard and two years of trying for another child, God blessed them with a baby boy, Josiah James. Although Missy and James were each living out their dreams, this also began a time of marital struggle for them. James was working through some personal issues, and Missy's lack of compassion and disrespect for him became the basis for their trouble. Missy was busy caring for the children and James was preparing to deploy to Iraq, but they wisely sought counsel from their pastor. They continued in counseling until James's deployment.

After ten months of counseling, the couple was making good progress, so they were disappointed when the time came for James to go overseas. But God used James's yearlong deployment to heal their marriage. As God worked to grow their love for Christ—and for one another—they missed each other terribly.

*Once Missy realized she needed to repent for her own contribution to their marital strife, she stopped blaming James for her lack of joy.*

Missy realized she didn't know how to be a good wife, so she began daily listening to radio programs that taught a biblical perspective on marriage, such as *Focus on the Family* and *Family Life Today*. "I became a student of marriage," she said. As she applied God's truth to her marital problems, she began to realize how wrong she had been in blaming James for her unhappiness. Once Missy realized she needed to repent for her own contribution to their marital strife, she stopped blaming James for her lack of joy. And God restored in Missy a deep love for her husband.

## HOME!

When James returned from Iraq, he and Missy had a new adoration and respect for each other. They recommitted to enjoying each other and determined to go out on a date at least once a month—something they had stopped doing after their second child was born.

Missy thanked God for James's deployment, because afterward they enjoyed some of the best years of their marriage.

When James was accepted to train with an airline, he told Missy it was another dream come true. Although she knew the job would mean long periods of James being away from home, Missy applied what she had learned and kept her mouth shut. Rather than nagging James, she took her concerns to God.

James quit the training when he realized he would be home only three days out of each month. "I just can't do that!" he told Missy.

She was so thankful she had waited for God to lead her husband to make the right decision. "When James made that decision, I felt so special that he chose us over his lifelong career dream."

Although James's decision meant Missy had to go back to work to help provide for the family while he waited for a pilot job opportunity, Missy was happy to have him home.

## LIVING THE DREAM

When the sheriff's department hired James to pilot their small plane, he was elated. The job allowed him to help the sheriff "chase the bad guys," as James put it, fly eight hours per shift, and be home each night.

Life was wonderful. Each day when James left for work Missy would say, "You leavin' now?" James would take her in his arms, give her a kiss, and say, "I'm never leaving!" Then he would kiss the kids, go fly his plane, and catch the bad guys.

One evening while James was working, Missy and the kids were at church. She had just settled the children in the class where she volunteered when the pastor's wife came to get her.

Missy remembers she looked distressed, and Missy's concern grew when the woman said, "Your friend is going to walk with us to the pastor's office."

When the friend approached she, too, looked distressed. As Missy was trying to figure out what was the matter, she never dreamed what would happen next. The pastor's office was filled with officers from the sheriff's department.

Missy remembers, "I began to go numb and just quietly say no-no-no."

The sheriff sat Missy down and explained James's plane had crashed. Neither James nor his partner had survived.

Missy recalls, "My mind raced back and forth between two thoughts. *I'm a widow. What about the kids?* I was in complete and utter shock. I was trembling as I heard people talking to me. They were asking who I wanted them to call. It didn't seem real. I felt like I was up in the air looking down on someone else's life."

## HOME ALONE

Missy's friend drove her and the children home, and a few people from church came to sit with them until her parents arrived.

Missy told me, "Our kids were ten and six years old, and I had to tell them their daddy had died. It was the hardest thing I've ever had to do. The following days were spent in total shock. A lot of it was just a blur. I was heartbroken, and so were my kids."

But God didn't leave Missy and the children to grieve alone. He showed up in amazing ways. For example, one night while tucking ten-year-old Jayleen into bed, Missy was amazed when amid her sobs her daughter sat up and calmly said, "This is really sad, Mom, but I know God has a plan for all of this."

God gave them strength when they recalled James's favorite Bible verse: "I know the plans I have for you…plans to prosper you and not to harm you, plans to give you hope and a future" (Jeremiah 29:11 NIV).

God continued to show Himself faithful as Missy's church family and MOPS (Mothers of Preschoolers) group provided prayer, emotional support, meals, childcare, and lawn and house maintenance. Her financial concerns were relieved when funeral expenses were donated, and the sheriff's department raised funds to meet various personal needs for the family.

Many nonbelievers heard the gospel at James's funeral, and Missy's friend read a lovely farewell letter Missy wrote to James. In the letter's closing, Missy said,

> Now that you've gone to be with our Lord in heaven, I am left again with a giant hole in my heart. I will truly miss you so much. Someone commented to me that you and I made a great team and it made me smile—because we really were an awesome team…You have left such an enormous legacy; the kids and I will surely do our best to continue your legacy of living life to the fullest, loving God and loving people.

## HOMECOMING

Learning to live without James has not been easy, but God gives their family strength. Throughout their 15 and a half years of marriage, Missy—and later the kids—had often waited for James's homecoming. Missy told me, "Now James is in our eternal home, and it is we who are on 'deployment' as ambassadors for Christ. And because of our hope in our Savior, it is James who awaits our homecoming."

## PONDER THIS

When God writes your love story, happily ever after may not always turn out the way you planned. For Missy, God had stirred in her heart a desire to marry a pilot, yet he also had prepared her as a young girl for the possibility of one day becoming a widow.

When Missy met James, she could easily have excused the fact that he was not a Christian. It would have been tempting to date him anyway when, out of the blue, James, a pilot, walked into her life. But Missy knew God's Word and applied biblical principles to her decision, rather than relying on circumstances that may have been interpreted as "a sign from God" by someone less discerning.

*When God writes your love story, happily ever after may not always turn out the way you planned.*

In the end, Missy's resolve not to date James when he wasn't a believer is what God used to draw James to Himself.

## ASK YOURSELF

When James passed away without warning, Missy and her children's initial response was to turn to the Lord. Because of their faith in Him, trust in His Word, and godly guidance from pastors and friends, they were able to keep their eyes fixed on Jesus when the unthinkable happened. Consider how you might respond to such tragedy.

Are you preparing yourself now for whatever God allows to come your way? First Peter 4:12 says, "Beloved, do not think it strange concerning the fiery trial which is to try you, as though some strange thing happened to you."

Whether you find yourself amid a storm or life is going rather well, you would be wise to follow Missy's example. Grow in your understanding of God's loving character so you will find His strength and help in time of need.

Let us therefore come boldly unto the throne of grace,
that we may obtain mercy
and find grace to help in time of need.
Hebrews 4:16

# 7

# The Single-Parent Club

## Matt and Dawn

Dawn was in her early twenties when she was swept off her feet by the most charming man she'd ever met. After a whirlwind romance, the two were married. Dawn was convinced she had found her happily ever after.

Over the next few years Dawn experienced great joy in the birth of her two daughters, Kaitlynn and Haley, and deep sorrow in the loss of two children through miscarriage. Amid this season of loss, Dawn recalls, "We knew something was missing in our lives. My husband started going to church, but because of a negative religious experience I had as a child, I didn't want anything to do with religion."

The more Dawn resisted the gospel, however, the more she wrestled with questions about the purpose of life. Eventually she agreed to go to church with her husband. It wasn't long before they both surrendered their hearts to Christ.

As they settled into Christian life, the two of them became involved in church. They were committed to learn more about God and how Christ's love could help them love each other.

### OUT OF NOWHERE

And then Dawn's life took a turn she never could have expected.

"On our tenth anniversary, everything seemed fine. But the day after, my husband told me he didn't love me anymore and he wanted a divorce. My knees buckled and I nearly fell to the floor."

Dawn could not believe what she was hearing. It had to be a dream. She couldn't wrap her mind around the words she'd just heard.

When her husband packed his things and moved out of their home, Dawn was stunned as the reality set in. Weeping inconsolably was her initial response. She couldn't begin to imagine how she would survive. And she worried about how the situation would affect her young daughters.

As the weeks passed, Dawn discovered within herself a strength she had never known. Her own strength? No. Dawn knew the power she was being given each day was coming from her relationship with the Lord. "The Lord gave me His strength every day to get out of bed and to take care of the needs of my children. And on the days I couldn't function, He sent godly women to help."

None of us can prepare ourselves for the betrayals we may face in life. But amid that incredible storm, Dawn's lifeline was in knowing Jesus and having His Holy Spirit guide her through Bible reading, prayer, and godly counsel.

When Dawn realized her husband was gone for good, she also realized her once comfortable life had been rocked to its core—never to be the same again. With her new life as a single mom came financial struggles and fear over how she would make ends meet. But over and over God showed Dawn He was nearby, meeting her needs in miraculous ways.

Dawn said, "I look back now and see so much of the Lord's love, faithfulness, and provision. I didn't always recognize His hand back then, but in hindsight I see it very clearly."

Dawn's parents lived a long distance away, so she leaned heavily on her Christian friends, who provided her little family with comfort and joy. Dawn and her girls learned a lot about God's character and love by how well they were loved by His people. As Dawn surrounded herself with godly girlfriends, she found the help she needed to move forward in her new life as a single mother. Sure, she cried herself to sleep at night, but she knew God was right there with her when she felt alone and destitute.

Dawn was determined not to allow her circumstances to destroy her.

If God really was her heavenly Father, she knew she could trust Him to work all things together for good in her painful situation. She was equally determined to pray for her daughters' love for Christ to grow.

As Dawn's heart gradually began to heal, she learned how to be happy again. Only now her happiness didn't lie in her comfortable circumstances. Rather, she discovered a new kind of joy that brought peace even when life didn't make sense. Dawn's daughters also learned genuine joy as God healed their hearts too.

Dawn said, "I tried to teach my daughters not to use this time in their life as a reason to fall away from Christ. Rather, we clung to James 1:2-5: 'Consider it pure joy, my brothers and sisters, whenever you face trials of many kinds, because you know that the testing of your faith produces perseverance. Let perseverance finish its work so that you may be mature and complete, not lacking anything. If any of you lacks wisdom, you should ask God, who gives generously to all without finding fault, and it will be given to you'" (NIV).

## FORGIVING WAS HARD; RESENTMENT WAS HARDER

God did grant Dawn His wisdom. She learned that God wanted her to forgive all the hurts from her broken marriage so He could grow her more into the image of Christ. Forgiving was hard, but hanging on to resentment was even harder because the Holy Spirit would not allow Dawn to continue in her sin of unforgiveness.

When Dawn finally took responsibility for her own contribution to her broken marriage and started to forgive her ex-husband, she began to grow in ways she never could have imagined. With God's help, Dawn let go of the need to put the blame solely on her ex-husband.

*Forgiving was hard, but hanging
on to resentment was even harder.*

For two years she worked through her insecurities, issues of betrayal, and unforgiveness. She regularly received godly counsel and was involved in several Bible studies. She kept close to godly older women who wouldn't let her hold on to grudges and who held her accountable whenever she was tempted to give up.

## THE SINGLE-PARENT CLUB

Matt was the single father of a four-year-old son named Eric. He had never married Eric's mom, who left when their child was only a year old. Matt considered it a blessing to have custody of his only son.

When Eric was two, Matt began to feel responsible to teach his son about God. But Matt knew very little about God or the Bible. As the Lord began to draw him to a desire to know more about Christ, he started visiting the church where Dawn and her daughters attended.

For the first time in his life, Matt understood how he could have a personal relationship with Jesus. When God convicted Matt of his need for a Savior, he didn't hesitate to surrender his life to Christ. As Matt began to grow in his new faith, he found himself attending Bible study with Dawn.

Matt was aware of Dawn's situation, and from afar he observed how deeply wounded she had been. Matt was also impressed by the way Dawn and her daughters relied on Christ for their strength.

Matt felt even more compassion toward Dawn when he learned how ill she had been with meningitis. When she was well enough to return to church, Matt made it a point to tell her he had been praying for her and to ask how she was feeling.

Dawn was touched by Matt's kind attention, but she was not at all thinking of him in a romantic way. Dawn remembers, "Neither of us was looking for anyone to date. We were both focused on our walk with the Lord and on raising our children."

In the beginning, Matt and Dawn's friendship developed out of their similar single-parenting experiences. When they both expressed their frustration over trying to find affordable childcare during working hours, they decided to help each other out. Dawn recalled, "My daughters were ages 11 and 9, and Matt's son was four years old. We needed help with babysitting, so we worked out a plan to help each other with day care."

Matt and Dawn were delighted by how well their children got along. Dawn's youngest daughter, Haley, and Eric developed a lovely bond. Whenever they were together Eric clung to Haley and she looked for ways to mother him.

Dawn found relief from financial pressure by sharing a house with a girlfriend who was also a single mom. Matt and Eric spent a lot of time there. Most nights the three families ate dinner together, and they often played games before Matt and Eric went home for the night. The bond that grew between their families reigned true to God's promise to place the lonely into families (Psalm 68:6).

At first both Matt and Dawn were guarded in how they felt toward each other. Dawn said, "Matt was aware I had severe trust issues, and he still stayed around. He was a single dad with his own issues, but we enjoyed the time we spent together, praying for each other and being a comfort in the midst of our healing."

## FIRST KISS

Dawn smiled as she recalled what happened one night after having dinner at her house. "Matt surprised me with our first kiss. He was so cute. We were saying good night like every other night, and he quickly snuck in a peck."

Dawn's heart fluttered over the sweet kiss. "It was in that moment that I knew I was falling in love with Matt."

Matt took things slow, but eventually he asked Dawn to go on an official date—just the two of them. Dawn accepted the invitation, but in her heart she was worried about stepping into a relationship with Matt that could either grow into a lifelong commitment or ruin their friendship. Both prospects terrified her. "We were both so nervous, like two high school kids on a first date."

Matt took Dawn to a nice restaurant, not the usual kid-friendly places both had become accustomed to. It was a nice change to carry on a conversation without little ears listening in or with the countless interruptions that come with dining with children.

As Matt and Dawn talked, they shared their insecurities about being in a relationship. Somehow being able to talk to each other about their concerns helped each of them grow in trust with the other.

By the time they finished dinner, they began to believe God would have them pursue a relationship. But they wanted to seek godly counsel, so they decided to meet with their pastor.

The pastor helped them talk about some of the issues from their past relationships they would need to work through. And he encouraged them to be careful to honor the Lord in their dating relationship so they would be led by His Spirit to discern if they should marry. He also reminded them that their children would be learning how to one day honor God in their own dating lives by watching their parents' dating relationship.

## I CHOOSE YOU

While they dated, Dawn often struggled with insecurities. Matt would gently remind her, "Babe, I choose you." His response helped to ease Dawn's fears and grow her trust in him even more.

Their dating life mostly consisted of church activities and family time with their combined three children—and they wouldn't have wanted it any other way. They knew if they were to marry they would be blending their families, so they wanted their kids to feel involved in the growth of their relationship.

After three years of courtship, the couple were married in a beautiful outdoor garden wedding. That day Matt, Dawn, and the kids became a blended family. I remember visiting with Eric at their wedding reception. I told him how fun it was that his mother now had the same last name as his father. He smiled, and then said, "And does that mean I now have to change my last name to be the same as my new sisters?"

I had to laugh at Eric's response. He was trying so hard to comprehend how his dad's marriage to Dawn would affect his own little life. Eric was excited to have a new mom, since he had never known his own mother, yet he was also apprehensive about sharing his father with a bunch of women who would be moving into their home.

Dawn and Matt have now been married almost ten years. Dawn's daughters are grown and both follow Christ. Eric is in high school and continues to grow into a young man who loves Jesus. Blending two families into one is always a challenge. Dawn told me, "Our blended family goes through trials and sometimes doesn't feel so blended. But in those times the Lord grows and refines us to the people He wants us to be." Dawn admits she still battles with insecurity, but whenever Matt says, "Babe, I picked you," he brings her right back to where she needs to be.

Dawn continued. "Matt says, 'I picked you,' but I know it was God who picked us for each other. We are polar opposites, yet God uses our differences to bring balance to our lives. Only God could have brought the two of us together."

## PONDER THIS

Watching someone's life fall apart is never easy. With divorce comes so much pain. But oh, how wonderful when God uses the pain to grow the faith of His children.

I don't believe God wants any of His people to divorce, but you and I both know Christians divorce despite God's desire that they stay committed to their covenant.

How should we respond to the divorced and single parents God brings to our churches? All too often divorced singles feel judged and unwelcome in churches. Does Jesus want us to ignore them? I think not.

Remember how in John chapter 4 Jesus intentionally went through Samaria because He had a divine appointment with the woman at the well—a woman who had been married five times and was scorned by her community? Jesus met her at the point of her need and showed her He was the answer she was searching for.

The woman was amazed when she declared, "He told me all that I ever did" (John 4:39 ESV). She was in awe that Jesus knew all about her and yet valued her as a person, so much so that He offered her "living water."

Let's follow Jesus's example. Let's look beyond the divorced person's past and offer them the gospel with genuine love. And for single-parent families, let's show them Christ's love by including them in our fellowships and outings.

ASK YOURSELF

Are you prepared to face a storm? In Matthew 14:22 we see that Jesus sent the disciples into a storm while He stayed ashore. As the disciples battled the waves, do you think they wondered why Jesus was not there in the boat with them? I know I would have.

When Jesus came to rescue them, He was walking on the water. Peter walked out on the water toward Jesus. In the same way, sometimes God allows storms so we'll learn to trust Him in ways we've never imagined, and to grow our faith so, like Peter, we will step out of the security of our boat to face the unknown with our eyes fixed on Jesus. But when Peter's faith faltered and he started to sink, Jesus reached out to save him.

While unexpected trials are never what you hope for, can you ask God to prepare you now to trust Him when a storm comes? Like Dawn who found strength from James 1:2-5, hide God's Word in your heart now so you won't sin against Him in times of trouble. I promise you won't regret it!

8

## A Time to Grow

### Sean and Allison

Sean had always dreamed of playing professional golf, so he devoted as much time as possible to studying under a golf pro while working odd jobs to pay the bills. One day while he was driving to work, he happened upon a radio station that was sharing the gospel of Jesus Christ. As the radio host explained that all have sinned and need a Savior, God opened Sean's understanding, and right there on the 405 freeway he prayed to receive Christ as his Savior and Lord.

"I was a brand-new Christian," Sean told me. "I knew I had given my life to God, but I didn't know what it meant to be a Christian. I didn't go to church—rather, I filled my time with work and volunteering for various causes."

One day a woman Sean worked with invited him to her church for Easter Sunday, and he agreed to go. Once Sean was in the building, however, he didn't feel as though he belonged there. "I wanted to serve God and grow, but I felt completely out of place."

But that morning the church choir performed a beautiful Easter cantata, and Sean was moved by the music and its message.

### MUSIC TO HIS EARS

In a moment, everything changed. Allison stepped up to the mic to sing a solo. Sean reminisces about that day. "The song was really powerful and spoke to me about the grace of our God. I felt drawn to her because I wanted to understand that grace more."

Sean decided to regularly attend that church and learn more about God's grace. While looking for a place to connect with this new Christian community, he decided to join the choir. It was a large group of people, but Sean immediately felt comfortable and welcome because they made him feel as though he was part of a big, loving family.

Because Allison was part of the choir community, Sean got to see how she interacted with others. "When I first met Allison, she was kind of this larger-than-life personality. She knew everybody at the church, and she was well loved there."

Sean admired Allison's fun-loving qualities, but he wasn't looking for a relationship. "At the time I didn't think God had marriage in store for me because I felt like I had lived a terrible life as a womanizer—and because of the things I had done in my past. I didn't think being a family man, a father, or a husband was in the cards for me. A relationship with a woman just wasn't on my radar. I really just wanted to get to know God and understand what He had for me to do while I was on this earth."

As Sean grew in his walk with Christ, he sought out godly men to disciple him.

All the while he and Allison continued to fellowship in the same circle of friends. When Sean began to sense he was attracted to Allison, he was hesitant to act on his feelings. He felt he had a lot of growing to do in his walk with Christ, and he was convinced Allison would be looking for someone who was a strong spiritual leader.

"One of the things that made me hesitant," he shared, "was that Allison had a five-year-old son. I had always said I was not going to have a 'microwave-ready family.' And I still felt very insecure in my faith and my spiritual maturity. I didn't think she would want to date someone like me, or that I could be any kind of father to her son. So I was very hesitant."

Allison chimed in. "When I met Sean at church, I thought he was a nice guy, but I wasn't interested. I thought he was younger than me, and I thought he seemed kind of shallow. I didn't really think he was my type anyway." Allison laughed as she said, "I didn't think he was very good-looking, which is so funny to me now because he is *incredibly* good-looking! God had serious blinders on me for sure."

## WOUNDED AND GUARDED

Allison had her own story of searching for Christ. She grew up in a loving Christian home, but she didn't have a relationship with Jesus until about a year before she met Sean. She was divorced and a single mom. She lamented, "I had messed my life up pretty badly and was living the consequences of those decisions, and it was hard."

Allison had become involved in church and devoted herself to pursuing Christ through Bible study, prayer, and fellowship with other believers. "This was all a very new, living, breathing relationship with Jesus that I had not known before."

Previously Allison had dated a man from church she thought she would marry. But he had ended the relationship quite abruptly a couple months before she met Sean. She was wounded, guarded, and uninterested in dating at all. She had determined her focus would be on being a good mom and leaning into her relationship with God.

*"I had messed my life up pretty badly and was living the consequences of those decisions, and it was hard."*

For about a year Sean and Allison continued to grow in their faith and fellowship with other believers. "Of course," Sean said, "I thought Allison was beautiful, and I thought she was really funny and kind of goofy, and those things attracted me to her because I'm goofy and funny too. We spent a lot of time with friends, and I was impacted by how everyone who knew Allison loved her. This is one of Allison's gifts that I continue to love to this day—she can meet you and make you feel like you've been her best friend forever. She makes you feel comfortable, she makes you feel right at home, she listens well. It's an amazing characteristic that God has given her. The more I grew to appreciate Allison, the more I wanted to be close to her because she made me feel good about myself."

Over time Sean's heart was being drawn to Allison. But he was afraid to move on anything that was not God's plan for him, so he prayed, "God, if this is what You want for me, You have to make it really clear."

## YOU'VE GOT MAIL

One Sunday morning Allison sang a solo in church that touched Sean's heart deeply. He wanted to thank her for the song and tell her how it moved him. He also wanted to let her know it was his birthday, but he felt embarrassed. It just seemed awkward at church in front of a bunch of people. So instead he got her email address from the church directory and sent her a nice little note of appreciation.

Soon Sean and Allison were emailing back and forth. They both felt it was a safe way to get to know each other without dating. But at this point Allison didn't know Sean had feelings for her. She just thought of him as a great friend.

The more they communicated through email, the more Sean's heart was being drawn toward Allison. One day he suggested in an email that they go out for a cup of coffee sometime. Allison agreed, but then Sean waited for a couple of months before calling her with an invitation. "I waited because I was scared and nervous, and didn't want to open that door if I wasn't ready to commit to being in a relationship with a woman who had a child."

About Sean's not calling, Allison added, "I figured he wasn't really interested in anything more than a friendship."

The more Sean prayed about the idea of pursuing Allison, the more he was sure God was putting in his heart a desire to pursue her. He didn't really know Allison very well, but he was determined it was time to get to know her better.

When Sean mustered up his courage and called Allison for a coffee date, she happily agreed to meet him. At the coffee shop they talked for almost five hours.

Sean was captivated by Allison. "It was amazing. I remember listening to her talk and laugh about her family and her faith and a little bit about her past. I left that night wanting to get to know her even more. I looked forward to the next time I could spend time with her. I just wanted to be close to her."

Allison said, "I remember leaving the coffee shop thinking, wow, there's a lot more to this guy than I thought." She chuckled. "And for the first time, I thought he was really cute!"

From that point on Sean and Allison looked for every opportunity they could find to get to know each other better.

Allison described that time. "We began a fast-track relationship. I don't know why, except that we were both really seeking what God had for us, and we both wanted a godly relationship. Neither of us had ever really experienced that. And we were both committed to building something that was lasting—not just fun for the moment. I felt protective of my son because I didn't want another man to come around and then leave again, and Sean was fully aware that he couldn't be in this halfhearted because of my son."

## WAIT FOR IT

Sean and Allison realized that during the time they waited to date God was growing each of them to be ready for what He had in store. After a month of dating, they were both thinking about marriage. But they wanted to honor the Lord in their courtship, so they surrounded themselves with godly friends and confidants who walked alongside them to provide accountability, godly counsel, and prayer.

Allison shared, "I can't even begin to describe how vital that community was to us during that time. We abstained from a sexual relationship, which was new for both of us. We had both lived promiscuous lives as adults, so building a relationship that did not involve sex was hard. It required immense trust in each other and in God. Abstinence built into our relationship a profound trust that would last a lifetime. We believed that if we could wait for each other, God would bless our marriage, our sex life, and the bond between us. I believed that if I could trust Sean to wait for me until our wedding day, then I could trust him to be faithful to me in our marriage—even when times got hard. And even more I learned that I could trust God to care for me too."

Soon Sean was certain Allison was the woman with whom he wanted to spend his life. Only five weeks from their first date, he bought a ring for her. But not only did he not give it to her; he told no one of his plans to marry her. And he had no idea how he was going to propose, but he knew they were meant to be together, and he was determined to make her his bride.

Before Sean proposed to Allison, he mentioned his plans to the pastor who had become his mentor. He wanted him to do their premarital counseling and perform the ceremony.

Sean was surprised when his mentor asked him to put off the proposal until he could do some counseling with both Sean and Allison, before they got caught up in planning a wedding. Sean didn't understand why the pastor asked him to wait, but he trusted his wisdom and guidance and agreed to hold off.

Sean said, "So we started counseling, and we worked hard. That time of counseling was one of the best things we ever could have done for our marriage. It allowed us to do some really important work, to really make sure we were right for each other *before* planning a wedding. Through the counseling we grew a lot in our relationship, and I became even more sure that this was the woman God had picked for me."

Six weeks later the pastor gave Sean the green light, and he proposed to Allison on Christmas Eve. Three months later all their friends and family rejoiced as they watched God join them in holy matrimony. And Allison's son was overjoyed to have Sean as his forever daddy. Not long after they wed, Sean was given the honor of legally adopting their son.

Sean and Allison have been happily married for 15 years and are the proud parents of three sons. Allison said, "Today, we still use the tools we were given in that counseling. We continue to work at our relationship on a daily basis. Some things have gotten easier as we have been married longer and longer, but some things still require much work. We both remain committed to serving God and serving each other in our marriage, and in our everyday lives. We always desire growth in our personal relationships with God and press into that even when it's painful. We work at being thankful for the lavish gift that God has bestowed on us in each other, and we love being with each other and learning more and more about each other every day."

Allison concluded, "Man, I love this man! What a lucky girl I am."

## PONDER THIS

I must admit I got a little teary-eyed while I wrote this story. I have known Allison since she was a little girl. I remember praying over her with her parents as she rebelled against her Christian upbringing. I also remember celebrating the work God did in her heart when He brought her to genuine repentance.

*Even when they make a mess of their lives, God is ready to forgive and show mercy to anyone who will call on Him.*

When God brought Sean into Allison's life, we all watched in awe as He graciously did a work in both of their hearts to prepare them to serve Christ as husband and wife. God can draw to Himself those who are His and bring to repentance those who are not. And He can heal broken hearts and teach them to love in the way He designed true love for marriage.

## ASK YOURSELF

Are you praying for someone who has made poor choices? Don't lose heart. Do you find yourself living through the consequences of your own poor choices? Fret not. Even when they make a mess of their lives, God is ready to forgive and show mercy to anyone who will call on Him (Psalm 86:5).

Isaiah 55:7 says, "Let the wicked forsake his way, and the unrighteous man his thoughts; let him return to the LORD, and He will have mercy on him; and to our God, for He will abundantly pardon."

# 9

## Dreams Don't Come True for a Girl Like Me

### Byron and Tammy

I n the summer of 1985, Tammy moved from a charming town in Oregon to a small town in California's Central Valley. She was just 14, and everything in her longed to remain in her familiar surroundings. But she had not been given a choice in the matter.

Tammy arrived in California to live with her sister and her grandmother. She recalls the first time she met Byron. "He was just one of my sister's friends from high school. He was a nice boy from down the street who came over to help unload the moving van."

Byron came for dinner from time to time, and he and Tammy would enjoy lots of laughs and talks. Tammy liked spending time with Byron—the very first friend she made in California.

Tammy recalls thinking this older boy was good-looking, but she never really thought of him as more than a friend. Since Byron was older than Tammy, she thought he wouldn't be attracted to her, and so she focused on relationships with other boys.

It wasn't long before Tammy found herself pregnant with the baby of one of her young boyfriends. She remembers thinking, "I'm having this baby. I am going to be doing this all alone, but I am having this baby."

One day, when Tammy was walking home from school, Byron drove by in his car. To her surprise, he turned the car around and pulled up alongside her. Through the passenger window, he called out, "Hey! Get in."

Tammy remembers, "I was so happy to see Byron, so I didn't hesitate to jump into his car."

In Byron's humorous, tell-it-like-it-is manner, he told me he took one look at Tammy and joked, "Looks like you have a kid on the way. Who do I have to shoot?"

Tammy was relieved Byron commented on her belly bump right off so there was no awkwardness about the fact that she was pregnant.

Tammy mentioned she was craving McDonald's French fries. They didn't have a McDonald's in their small town, but Byron decided Tammy needed some special treatment that day. He drove with her for nearly two hours to Monterey Bay, to enjoy the ocean breeze *and* some delicious French fries.

Looking back, Tammy said, "I didn't take Byron's hint very well. I now realize he was taking me on a date that day. But since I thought of Byron as a good friend, I assumed that was how he viewed our relationship as well."

Although over the years the two remained friends, popping in and out of each other's lives, both Tammy and Byron married other people.

After going through her second divorce in October 2010, Tammy was at the lowest point in her life. "I had two failed marriages. I was the mother of three children—by three different fathers—and I had no job. So I had to move in with my mother. I was very depressed. Here I was, a 39-year-old woman with nowhere to go, sleeping on the floor in my mother's house."

After being hurt deeply by the men in her life, Tammy officially wrote off *all* men—until one day she crossed paths with Byron, her trusted childhood friend. In his usual humorous fashion, he greeted her with, "Hello from the ghost of Christmas past!"

To hear from Byron after so many years was a breath of fresh air for Tammy. She was more than a little relieved to learn he was also single.

The two exchanged phone numbers, and when Tammy's phone rang, she was delighted to discover it was Byron calling. Tammy remembers how they talked for hours as they caught up on all that had gone on in each of their lives.

Tammy recalled one of Byron's most romantic gestures. "Byron was a truck driver—he still is—and he and I had a great phone conversation while he was in El Paso, Texas. By the end of the phone call, I guess Byron thought I needed a hug. Or maybe he needed one. Byron was training a new driver at the time, so between him and his driver-in-training, they drove 1400 miles without stopping just to get a hug from me." Tammy smiled as she said, "It was then that I knew I wanted to marry Byron."

Not knowing if Byron would ever want to marry her, she told him, "Whatever this relationship is, we are not going to throw in the towel. We are stuck with each other forever!"

While Byron was away driving, the couple spent hours and hours on the phone. One day he asked Tammy to come along with him on one of his routes. She was excited to have three long weeks to talk with Byron as he drove.

A couple of days before the trip came to an end, Byron stopped at a shopping mall so they could get out and stretch their legs. They happened upon a jewelry store. When Byron exclaimed, "Hey, let's look in here!" Tammy thought perhaps she was dreaming.

The next thing Tammy knew, she had found a ring she liked. Byron said a few words to the woman at the jewelry store and then dashed off to find an ATM machine, leaving Tammy alone in the store until he came back.

Byron promptly returned with cash in hand to purchase the ring that had caught Tammy's eye. The kind woman handed Byron the ring she had boxed up for him.

At the mall's food court, Tammy was enjoying some French fries when Byron took out the ring, got down on one knee, proclaimed his love for her, and asked her to be his wife—right there in the mall!

## A GIRL LIKE ME

Of course Tammy said yes, and soon they were making wedding plans. All the while, Tammy was troubled with thoughts like, *This is not going to work out. Dreams like this never come true for a girl like me.* Another issue that bothered Tammy was that Byron had professed to be a Christian, and she was not interested in such things.

But Tammy's concerns were put to rest when she and Byron married in September 2011—26 years after she and Byron first met when they were teens.

Tammy said, "So we were married. But I was still sleeping on the floor of my mom's house for weeks at a time while Byron was away driving."

## A PLACE TO CALL HOME

Two months later, Byron's father called Tammy to come over to his house. It was in the same town where she was living. After being widowed for several years, Byron's father had recently remarried as well (coincidently, to his own high-school sweetheart!).

Byron's dad told Tammy he was moving into his new wife's home. With that, he handed her the keys to his home—the same home where Byron had grown up. Tammy's father-in-law said, "This is the key to your house now. This house is now yours and Byron's. Enjoy it. I love you."

Tammy could hardly believe it! Not only had she married the most wonderful man she had ever known, but now she and Byron would have a house to live in—a home where they could grow old together.

Tammy and Byron settled into their new life together in their charming house which happened to be across the street from a Baptist church. Byron was always away working on Sundays, but each week Tammy watched the activity at the little church.

When Tammy's daughter, Lesley, came to live with her and Byron, Lesley began to attend church on Sundays. Tammy didn't go with her, and she remembered being irritated that Lesley took so long to come home after church was over.

Week after week, Tammy watched many of the people stay and visit long after the service had dismissed. This type of fellowship made no sense to Tammy, and she didn't think Lesley should be wasting so much time over there.

Meanwhile, Byron was enjoying great fellowship with the Lord. He had become a truck-stop pastor, delivering sermons on Sunday mornings at various truck stops along his route. Byron had been raised in a Christian home, and the foundation he had from those bringing-up years stirred in him a desire to serve the Lord while he was on the road.

All the while, Byron was praying for the Lord to open Tammy's eyes to her need for a Savior.

One Christmas Lesley invited her mother to come to a ladies' Christmas cookie exchange at the church. Tammy thought the event didn't sound too threatening, so she agreed to go.

The cookie exchange was where I first met Tammy. I had the honor of sharing the gospel at the event, and it wasn't long before Tammy and I were conversing through social media. She had a lot of questions about Christianity, and she wanted to know more about the free gift of salvation.

In the many years my husband, Steve, and I have been in ministry, the story of Tammy's conversion is one of our favorites. Ever since the Lord helped her see the need to repent of her sins and surrender her life to Jesus as her Lord and Savior, there's been no stopping her! Her life has been forever transformed, and she beams with joy over the new life she found in her relationship with Jesus.

> *No matter how much you or I complicate our*
> *lives, God is still sovereign over our mess.*

The first time we met Byron, he was bigger than life. He was beyond excited that his wife had come to Christ, and he could hardly believe God used the little church across the street to draw her to repentance.

Over 26 years ago, God knew Byron and Tammy would be His. In His kindness, He allowed them to meet as children, and then providentially crossed their paths again when Tammy was at the lowest point of her life. Not only did God prepare them for each other, but He prepared their hearts to love and serve Him as well. Tammy said, "God knew what He was doing back in June of 1985."

These days Byron and Tammy are happily married, deeply in love, and the best of friends. Hand in hand and with eyes on Jesus, they have walked together through some of life's painful consequences. Through it all, the joy of the Lord has certainly been their strength.

Knowing the sweet love story of Byron and Tammy, I was delighted on their anniversary to see Byron proclaim his love on social media in a post that read, "Who else would drive you to Monterey for French fries?"

## PONDER THIS

Tammy and Byron's love story teaches us that no matter how much you or I complicate our lives, God is still sovereign over our mess. How kind is our God to draw to Himself those who will be His.

Romans 8:28 promises, "All things work together for good to them that love God, to them who are the called according to his purpose" (KJV).

No matter how hopeless a person may feel, with God there is always hope for anyone who will bow their knee, ask His forgiveness, and surrender their life to Jesus.

## ASK YOURSELF

Maybe you, like Tammy, find yourself in a desperate situation. Looking to yet another man to fill the ache in your heart will never bring you the happiness you long for. Romans 5:8 says, "God demonstrates His own love toward us, in that while we were still sinners, Christ died for us."

God created you to find your worth in a relationship with Him. Ask yourself if you've been searching for happiness in disappointing relationships. If so, let today be the day you turn from finding your worth in how others treat you, to discover how very much you are treasured by your creator.

# 10

# The Secret

## Chuck and Angie

Angie was in high school when she made the commitment to not date for six months. By the middle of her senior year, her walk with the Lord had become extremely important to her, and she knew her preoccupation with the opposite sex was a distraction.

God had brought Angie through some difficult experiences as a child, and she was fully aware of His hand of protection and guidance in her life. How could she do anything but serve Christ after all He had done for her?

But Angie wasn't just "not dating." She was searching the Bible to discover what type of man God would have for her in the future. As she read she became hopeful that God would lead her to a man who loved Jesus even more than she did. She prayed for God to lead her to "the one" who would be passionate in his walk with the Lord and bold about sharing his faith with others.

Angie wasn't looking for the love she'd seen portrayed in movies. She wanted a love rooted and grounded in Christ. She yearned for someone with whom she could serve the Lord for their whole lives.

Divorce would not be an option; of that Angie was certain. She had grown up watching the pain of divorce and was resolved to be married to her one true love—forever.

Patience is rarely the defining quality of a teenage girl, but Angie prayed for God to give her patience to wait for Him to bring the man of her dreams. She prayed, *God, just let me meet him. I don't even have to know it's him, and we don't even have to start dating as soon as my commitment to not date has ended. I just want to know him.*

## TRUE LOVE WAITS

In February of that year, Angie joined her church's youth group to attend True Love Waits, a conference that teaches teens and young adults the importance of obeying God's command to enjoy sex only in marriage. Angie was excited to attend the conference because she would hear great speakers and meet thousands of others who would join her in a commitment to keep themselves pure.

Angie attended a public school where many girls her age were sexually active, making her feel as though she was the only one waiting. She knew there were others, but most girls were private about their resolve to wait. Angie was tired of being private. She wanted to be bold about her decision to honor Christ with her purity!

The conference did not disappoint. Thousands of teens and young adults proclaimed their promise to remain pure. Each high school and college student was given a commitment card to fill out. Then they were challenged to take their signed covenant card to school and post it on a stake in the ground on the school's lawn.

Angie was excited to post her card along with many others at school the next day. She was encouraged to see the number of students who were as committed to purity as she was. Their bold statement made their commitment evident to everyone who passed the cards, even though it rained and all the cards got wet—except one someone had the foresight to wrap in plastic.

Angie could hardly wait to go back to the conference again that evening. It was Valentine's Day, and while so many of the couples at school were showing their affection for each other, Angie knew her affection for Christ was shining through, and she was happy to know she wasn't alone.

This conference was different from any other Angie had attended. In the past she would have been more interested in trying to meet boys than she was in listening to what the Lord might want to teach her. This time her motive was right, and without any distractions she was learning just what she needed to know.

After a wonderful time of worship, there was an intermission before the sermon. Thousands of people left their seats to visit the concession stands, and Angie was no exception. As she made her way back into the stadium, she found herself walking behind a young man wearing a Promise Keepers baseball cap and a T-shirt with a Christian message. Angie thought, *Wow, that guy wore all that to his school today? He must be unashamed of Christ.*

Angie was impressed with his boldness, and she found herself praying, *God, I want a man like that. One who will be bold about his relationship with You. One who will be united with me about following You. I want us to be a team for You.*

Just before the young man disappeared into the massive crowd, two of her girlfriends approached her. As one friend reached to give Angie a hug, the other called out to the guy she had been eyeing. "Hey, Chuck!"

Chuck turned around to greet his friend. Angie was amazed as she considered the coincidence of her friends approaching at that very moment, and that in a sea of three thousand people Chuck happened to be their friend.

The group began chatting, and Angie tried not to be distracted by how cute she thought Chuck was. When she mentioned that one girl had been smart enough to cover her purity covenant card with plastic, Chuck responded, "Yeah, that was my youngest sister, Tammy. My sister Melanie did the same thing on our college campus."

When Chuck mentioned Mitsi, his third sister, Angie could hardly believe Chuck had three sisters and that Angie knew all of them! She was surprised the sisters had never told her they had a brother. That day Angie learned Chuck lived in the same community she did, and that he was a youth leader for a church in their community.

When the event ended Angie went home thinking their chance meeting was unusual. But when a friend told her Chuck had a girlfriend, she put him out of her mind. Besides, she was still trying to keep her commitment to not date until the end of that school year.

After Angie's "dating fast" had ended, she still resolved not to start looking for a boyfriend. She had enjoyed the relief of not thinking about guys, and her walk with God had never been sweeter.

That summer after graduation, Angie's family decided to leave the church where she had been involved. She agreed with their reasons for looking for another church, but the decision shook her to the core. She resolved to seek God's leading for where He would have her serve Him.

By now Angie was working at a summer job, and she had become friends with a coworker named Tony. When she shared with him that she was looking for a new church, Tony said, "My parents are in youth ministry. We have youth group at our house each week. You should come."

Tony was a great guy, so she thought it might be fun to visit his church. The first night she attended youth group, Angie knew she had found a place to belong.

And then as Angie surveyed the chaos of 200 teenagers converging on the youth pastor's house, her eyes caught a glimpse of Chuck! She prayed, *Oh no. Dear God, please don't let him be a distraction. I don't want him to be the reason I come to this church.*

When Angie remembered Chuck had a girlfriend, she was relieved to enjoy her newfound church family without feeling distracted by trying to get Chuck to notice her. Soon Angie's family joined the church, and she was delighted. The teaching was sound, and the people were passionate to share the gospel, to love God, and to love others. She was home.

Angie grew to be good friends with Chuck's sister Melanie. They were in the same season of their lives, and they had the same desire to love and serve the Lord. Angie was regularly attending youth group and the church's college Bible study as well. It wasn't long before she was asked to become a youth leader with Melanie, Chuck, and several other young adults.

As Angie was keeping her eyes on Jesus, she couldn't help but observe how Chuck interacted with others. She knew him to be humble and kind in all facets of life. Secretly Angie was weighing out Chuck's actions. She thought, *Does he honor his parents? Does he care for his sisters? Is he honest?* He was constantly passing the test.

The more Angie got to know Chuck, the better she liked him. When she learned he had broken up with his girlfriend, she was excited. And when she heard he had broken off the two-and-a-half-year relationship on Valentine's Day because of a sermon he heard at the conference, she was impressed. Not only at Chuck's obedience to the Lord's prompting, but also because that was the very day Angie met him.

Angie laughed. "I joked that Chuck became single because he met me, but really he was just being obedient to God."

Once Angie realized Chuck was available, she had to rethink how she would interact with him. "Sometimes I flirted with Chuck when I knew I shouldn't. But then other times I would treat him like a brother. Poor Chuck was totally confused."

Chuck didn't seem to be interested in stepping right into another relationship. He had broken off his relationship so he could better seek God's will for his life. Another girlfriend would likely be a distraction. But Chuck liked Angie a lot. Still, he was convinced she had put him in the "friend" category a long time ago.

And Angie still was not really looking for someone to date. "My approach to dating was not like the world dates, going from one guy to the next, trying to find someone who made me feel loved. Rather, I was depending on God for each step. Dating became less appealing, while the idea of marriage to someone with whom I could serve Christ became my calling."

## I WANNA HOLD YOUR HAND

For almost three years Angie and Chuck had great fun serving the Lord as youth leaders. They ministered to teens, took them to camp, mentored students, and led them in worship.

Chuck and Angie each sensed a growing affection for the other, but they kept their feelings to themselves. Chuck believed Angie thought of him as a friend, and Angie decided if God wanted them together Chuck would have to make the first move.

One day Chuck decided to see what would happen if he held Angie's hand. She was surprised and elated. A few days later he held her hand again. Nothing was said, but Angie knew it was time to have a serious conversation.

The next day, however, both Chuck and Angie left on separate vacations. For a week, each had time to think and pray about the next step for their relationship.

While camping with her family, Angie met a woman who said after years of marriage her husband left her for another woman. Angie's heart was gripped with fear. Her mind was bombarded with painful thoughts. *Maybe I'm not supposed to be with Chuck at all. Is God trying to warn me that this could happen to me? How can I know if we would have a successful marriage?*

The woman eased Angie's concerns by telling her to read Ephesians chapter 5, and to marry a man who loved her like Christ loves the church. As Angie read over Ephesians, she realized God could help them have a successful marriage.

By the end of Angie's week away from Chuck, she had decided she didn't want to date Chuck. She wanted to marry him!

Chuck had also done a lot of thinking and praying while he and Angie were apart, and he initiated a conversation with her one night after college group. Their talk was a long time coming. For years each had been pondering the idea of a relationship with the other. They laughed at how they had each sent the other mixed signals and how along the way they had confused each other about their intentions.

Days later Chuck asked Angie's father's permission to date her. Chuck's request came as a surprise to her dad because he thought the two were just friends, but he granted his blessing happily.

Two weeks later, Chuck and Angie realized dating for most people is to get to know someone to determine if they want to marry that person. Both agreed they already knew they should marry, so they said, "What are we waiting for?"

When Chuck went back to Angie's father to ask for her hand in marriage, he was shocked but also very happy for the couple. With that, they announced their engagement and were married four months later!

Angie could hardly believe God's faithfulness to bring to her a godly man to be her husband. All her fears were replaced with confidence, and her trust in Chuck was secure.

## NO SECRETS

During Chuck and Angie's short engagement period, they were committed to be completely honest with each other. Their motto was "no secrets." They went through six weeks of premarital counseling to expose anything they thought could negatively affect their marriage. You can imagine Angie's devastation when, well after their wedding, Chuck finally shared with her a secret he'd been keeping for many years.

Chuck was a computer geek. He went to college to train in a high-tech career and he spent a lot of time on the Internet. When he was young, searching the web was a new phenomenon, and few considered how it might influence an upcoming generation.

As a teen Chuck had stumbled upon pornography on the Internet. He wasn't the only one. Many young men Chuck's age were opening doors to temptations they didn't realize would grab hold of them for the rest of their lives.

Being raised in a Christian home, Chuck had been taught that God wanted him to wait for sex until he was married. In Chuck's immaturity, he convinced himself pornography was a way to "keep" himself from having sex until he wed. The more Chuck opened the door, however, the more it became apparent he could not easily close it. Although God convicted Chuck whenever he looked at pornography, he convinced himself it was not as bad as having sex outside of marriage.

Chuck never told Angie about viewing pornography because he'd been convinced that once he was married and enjoying sex with his wife, pornography would lose its hold on him. Boy, was he wrong.

After six months of marriage, Angie began to suspect something was not right in their relationship. With what little experience she had on the Internet, she stumbled across the root of Chuck's problem. She was devastated to discover he had been regularly looking at pornography. When Angie confronted him, he was ashamed and apologized. Angie was relieved when Chuck said, "Okay, I'll quit. No problem."

But it *was* a problem. Angie eventually realized Chuck's draw to porn was an addiction. The doors he had opened so many years ago would not let him go. Time after time Chuck repented and promised, but over and over again he found himself back at the computer.

Angie said, "Let's solve this by removing Internet access from our home." But that didn't resolve the heart of Chuck's problem. She reflected, "We were so clueless as to what steps to take to help Chuck with his addiction. We had a long road ahead of us to fight this battle together."

Chuck sought out a group of godly men to hold him accountable and to talk through the root problem of his addiction. Chuck was relieved to learn he was not alone in his battle, and he found great support from the men he met.

Angie had to work through her own feelings of insecurity and betrayal. She had put her trust in Chuck and he had let her down. The secrecy was almost more painful than the addiction. But Angie was committed to fight this battle alongside her husband. And fight she did—on her knees. Wrestling to take her thoughts captive whenever she dwelt on her disappointment in her husband was the hardest thing she had ever done, and yet it brought her the sense of peace and strength she needed. She joined women's Bible studies to continue her spiritual growth, and she sought counsel from other women who had walked a similar path.

> *Wrestling to take her thoughts captive whenever she dwelt on her disappointment in her husband was the hardest thing Angie had ever done.*

Forgiving Chuck was hard, but not resenting him was even harder. As Angie pressed into her love for Christ, He gave her His selfless love for Chuck. And as Chuck has allowed God's Spirit to strengthen him in his battle against his addiction, he has seen strides of great victory.

Angie gives this advice to any woman who finds herself in a similar situation: "What helped me was prayer. And humbling myself to realize that whatever sin I am addicted to is equal to Chuck's. And as much as I try to break free of my familiar sinful struggles, Chuck is working to break free from his."

When Angie stopped looking at herself as the victim but turned her eyes to Christ, asking Him to grant her His compassion, she found freedom from the insecurity she struggled with because of her husband's addiction to pornography. Seeking out reputable Christian sites that provide counsel for couples (such as Focus on the Family and the Association of Biblical Counselors) was a real help for Chuck and Angie. With help Angie no longer asked herself why she wasn't enough. Rather, she learned Christ is enough to heal her wounded marriage, enough to help them win their battle.

Chuck and Angie have been married 17 wonderful years. Each anniversary marks another year of them standing together against Chuck's addiction. Angie has come to understand how so many years ago it was God who prepared her to walk with Chuck through his struggle.

*"This hard-earned, willing-to-forgive, grace-filled love is far superior to anything I could have hoped for."*

"There is so much hope. So many good years. The God of all comfort has worked in my life in so many ways. We both have some battle scars, but I have learned to love the man God called me to with an ever-deepening love for who Chuck is—sin nature and all. And the most unexpected blessing is that he has reciprocated that love. I can confidently say he loves me sacrificially as Christ loves the church. I'm proud of Chuck, who fights for us when he daily battles his sin nature. This hard-earned, willing-to-forgive, grace-filled love is far superior to anything I could have hoped for."

## PONDER THIS

It was our son Tony who invited Angie to our youth group so many years ago. Steve was a youth pastor, and our house was constantly filled with teens and college students. I remember the day Angie first walked into our home. The Lord instantly knit my heart to hers. Meeting a teen who was so determined to serve Christ is always a breath of fresh air. And watching God knit together the hearts of Chuck and Angie was pure delight.

It's interesting to consider how God led Angie to Chuck despite his secret addiction. God prepared Angie and called her to stand alongside Chuck to battle with him in God's strength. God entrusted her with the ministry of helping Chuck break free from Satan's hold and deception.

Chuck did not intend to hurt Angie. He was convinced the shameful practice would be behind him once he married her. She was, after all, the love of his life. Maybe you're in a similar situation. If so, I pray you consider Angie's words of advice and follow Chuck's example to seek help. Sin is sin, no matter what you wrestle with. Whether it's a porn addiction or bitterness toward your spouse for his sin, it will keep you from joyfully serving Christ.

## ASK YOURSELF

Once a person surrenders to Jesus, God promises that person who was once dead is made alive, and that old things pass away for him or her to become a new creature in Christ (Romans 6:11; 2 Corinthians 5:17). However, believers are still saddled with fleshly cravings. We must each fight the battle between our flesh and the Spirit for the rest of our lives. How have you prepared yourself for the war against the flesh?

You're not alone in the battle. Victories come when you learn to fight with the weapons God provides. "The weapons of our warfare are not of the flesh but have divine power to destroy strongholds" (2 Corinthians 10:4 ESV).

God provides the sword of the Word to fight off Satan's schemes (Ephesians 6:17; Hebrews 4:12). And He gives us the power of prayer and each other to help fight the battle. "Confess your sins to one another and pray for one another, that you may be healed. The prayer of a righteous person has great power as it is working" (James 5:16 ESV).

*Victories come when you learn to fight*
*with the weapons God provides.*

It took courage for Chuck to share his story, but he has learned secrecy is not what God has for him. God is using Chuck and Angie's story to offer hope and healing to thousands of couples who fight the same battle. Please take a moment to pray for Chuck and Angie—and for others who war against similar addictions.

## 11

## *Love Survives Loss*

### Don and Barb

Barb was a single mom of two daughters when she worked as a nurse in a hospital emergency room in Huntington Beach, California. Although working there was extremely hectic, she was never too busy to notice the handsome police officer whose work often brought him to the ER.

Whenever Don visited the emergency room, he routinely helped himself to a cup of coffee available in the nurse's break room. While Don was thankful for the free cup of coffee, he was even more grateful for the kind smile he regularly received from Barb.

Barb was a pretty woman, but Don knew several lovely ladies. *Barb is different,* he thought. Something about her kindness and gentle eyes drew Don toward her. Over time he found himself looking forward to the next opportunity to see Barb at the hospital.

The more time Barb and Don spent talking, the more their hearts were drawn toward each other. Don said, "The aha moment for us was more of a journey than a particular point of realization. We just came to know we were meant to be together."

As Don and Barb began to spend time together outside of their work environment, Don fell more in love with Barb as he watched her lovingly care for her two daughters, Doreen and Colleen. Don grew to feel deeply connected to Barb and her children.

It wasn't long before the couple were married, and they were a family of four. Then they were blessed with a beautiful son named Jason.

## LIFE COULDN'T BE MORE PERFECT

*Life couldn't be more perfect*, Barb often thought. But all the while she was plagued with troubling dreams that caused her great distress.

Barb recalled, "For years I would dream that I was swimming in a lake with my two little girls. Suddenly both girls would start to sink and I was not able to reach both of them. I knew Doreen, the oldest, was strong enough to make it to shore, but Colleen would need my help. The dream ended there each time. As time passed, I would see Doreen lying in a cornfield where she was always alone."

Barb was a Christian, so she knew God was sovereign over the safety of her children. Yet the recurring dream caused her to hold back from totally surrendering herself and her children to the Lord.

Barb and Don regularly took their kids to church, but they each knew something was not right about their walk with Christ.

Barb knew her distrust of God's sovereignty was what was holding her back. One Sunday a guest speaker shared how God was using him to serve Christ. For some reason this man's story resonated with Barb and caused her to long to be used by the Lord as well.

She prayed, *Lord, I want to be used by You. Please help me to serve You.*

Instantly she heard God's voice convicting her heart. *Barbara, you know why I can't use you that way.*

Barb did know why God couldn't use her. She had often told him, *Father, please use me, but don't take my children.*

"I wanted to serve Him but was afraid that one of my children would be taken from me. I didn't trust my Savior with the precious gift of my children. As I sat there crying, I prayed again, *Father, I want what You want for my life and whatever it takes to take me there—I trust You.* I looked at my daughter and knew I had just given her back to her heavenly Father. I thought the tears would never stop!"

Although Barb was tearful, she was no longer fearful. God's Holy Spirit had granted her the peace that surpasses understanding, and she now looked forward to the way God might use her for His kingdom purposes.

Not long after Barb's transforming surrender, Doreen went forward in church to rededicate her life to Christ. Barb was beyond grateful that her own surrender to the Lord's will had profoundly influenced her daughter's desire to be used by God as well. "A chill came over me, but I couldn't help but thank God because He showed me how much He loved Doreen and that He would take care of her."

That day Barb's faith started to grow greatly. God helped her conquer her fears as He assured her that she could trust Him completely.

About six months later Colleen was babysitting. She was hungry, so she called Doreen to do her a favor and bring over a burger and fries. It was nine o'clock at night when Doreen asked Barb if she could borrow her car to run dinner over to her sister. Barb thought it was rather late and suggested she not go, but Doreen responded, "It's okay, Mom. I really don't mind."

When Colleen arrived home from babysitting, she told Barb Doreen never arrived with her dinner. Barb attempted to calm her nerves as she sat at the table with a cup of tea, reading her Bible. It was out of character for Doreen to be away so long without checking in. This was before cell phones, so Barb had no way to reach Doreen. All she could do was wait—and pray.

Around midnight Barb knew something was terribly wrong, and panic began to set in.

## THE PHONE CALL

Then the phone rang. Barb's heart sank when the voice on the other end of the line was not Doreen, but someone explaining that Doreen had been in a serious accident. Barb needed to get to the hospital immediately.

Barb felt completely helpless. Doreen had taken her car and Don was an hour away at work, so she didn't even have a way to drive to the hospital to be with her daughter. The hospital assured Barb they would send over a highway patrol car to pick them up.

On the way there Barb, Colleen, and Jason could hardly speak, but they quietly prayed for Doreen.

As they walked into the hospital emergency room, a doctor met them at the door. Barb instinctively thought, *He wouldn't be out here talking to me if Doreen was still alive.* Her heart seemed to stop as the doctor led them to her room.

Doreen was with Jesus.

Barb called Don at work and said only that Doreen had been in an accident. He had a long drive to the hospital, and she didn't want him to know the worst of the news.

When Don received the phone call, he immediately notified his supervisor and left. He made it to the hospital in less than an hour, but when he got there, Barb told him it was too late. He went in to see Doreen, but his grief was so great that he couldn't stay there for very long. He went to the parking lot and walked up and down it for almost an hour, cursing God for taking his daughter. Several people tried to console him, but he wouldn't listen to anyone.

## EVEN IN DEATH

Doreen was deeply loved by her family and friends, and her funeral was a well-attended celebration of a life well lived.

Barb was encouraged that Doreen's funeral had brought an opportunity to share with countless people the hope that they would see Doreen again because she had a relationship with Christ.

After the funeral Barb and Don were at home with close family and friends when a friend of Doreen's stopped by. The young man called Barb over to talk privately. He shared how Doreen's death had caused him to consider his own mortality. When he heard how sure others were that they would see Doreen again in heaven, he realized he had no such confidence. His questions led him into a discussion with his boss, who was a believer. That very day the young man had asked Jesus to be his Savior.

Barb could hardly believe how God used Doreen for His kingdom purposes—even in her death. When the young man left, Barb recounted his story to their family and friends. They all celebrated God's goodness and talked of how sweet it would be to one day see Doreen in heaven.

## WILL I SEE HER AGAIN?

For most of Don's adult life he had professed to be a Christian, and yet when he heard everyone talking confidently of one day being in heaven with Doreen, he knew he didn't share their assurance.

> I began to isolate myself from the family for several months because I knew I had not accepted Jesus as my personal Lord and Savior. But I could not admit it because I had been living a lie for so long about knowing Him. I continued to go to church because I was expected to, but I really had no desire to be there and was still so angry at God for taking Doreen.
>
> Fortunately, the Holy Spirit continued to work on me, and about six months later, while sitting in the balcony on Sunday night, I finally listened to Him. The pastor had been talking about the forgiveness of Christ, and I knew that was what I needed in my life. That night I went forward and accepted Christ as my personal Lord and Savior. And then I confessed to my family that I had been living a lie all those years.

Through God's grace Don came to understand that God had forgiven all his sins, and that because he now had a genuine relationship with Jesus, he would one day go to heaven. And he was now confident that he would one day worship with Doreen before the throne of grace.

Barb and Don could hardly believe how Doreen's death had been the catalyst for Don to humbly admit he needed a Savior. Even in Doreen's death God continued to use her story to shine brightly for Christ.

Over the next few years Barb and Don had to work through the devastation of losing Doreen. Colleen struggled with feelings of guilt over asking Doreen to bring her dinner that fateful night. The more Colleen pulled away from them, the more Barb and Don worried they would lose her too.

Barb attempted to push away her grief by keeping herself busy. But she was also putting up walls that isolated her from Don and her children. "Hoping not to feel the pain, Don and I became involved in the singles ministry at our church—to keep ourselves busy. However, this took a tremendous toll on both of us. About a year later I started to fall apart and I withdrew. Don would start arguments with me to get me to open up. On one occasion, I blurted out, 'I just want to die.' I wasn't suicidal, just exhausted and depressed. But my response scared Don, so he called our pastor and we met the next morning."

## SEEK HELP

The pastor helped Barb to see how, although she had surrendered Doreen to the Lord, she had failed to surrender her grief to the Lord. She had been trying to work through her loss in her own strength. And she had taken upon herself the burden of trying to heal her family without God's help.

Again Barb was faced with the reality that God wanted her to surrender her family and their healing to Him.

As Barb and Don let go of their need to control the outcome of Doreen's death, the peace of God ruled in their hearts and minds. And rather than their grief causing strain on their marriage, it knit their hearts together in love for Christ and for each other like no other experience could have.

Losing Doreen was never something Barb wanted to happen. But looking back she can see how God prepared her to accept His plan to bring many to Christ through her death. And Don knows losing Doreen was the catalyst God used to bring him to realize he had never truly surrendered to Christ.

> *"Life brings about pain and struggle, but in Christ the
> pain brings growth and healing beyond belief."*

These days Barb and Don share their story with anyone God brings their way. Barb said, "It's been 31 years since our lives were changed forever. We will never stop loving Doreen nor will we stop missing her, but God has restored our family and healed the grief of our now adult children. Colleen and Jason are both married to wonderful spouses and are raising our wonderful grandchildren, whom we love deeply. Don and I have grown profoundly in our love for the Lord and for each other. We know we have been blessed beyond imagination."

She concluded, "Life brings about pain and struggle, but in Christ the pain brings growth and healing beyond belief. I would have preferred that He didn't allow Doreen to be taken from us, but I know she is with the Lord and we will all be united again someday, in His time and for His glory. In the meantime, God is using our story to encourage others and to glorify Christ."

## PONDER THIS

Wow. Right? Don and Barb's story certainly took my breath away. I don't know about you, but I can remember having a similar conversation with the Lord regarding the security of my own kids.

As I came to understand God's love for my children far exceeds my own love for them, I learned to trust Him with their future. That doesn't mean I never struggle with worry over their security, but the more I surrender them to His loving hand, the more at peace I become. Have you found this peace?

Does Don and Barb's story resonate with you because you have experienced an unexpected sorrow? Has your loss caused a rift between you and the Lord—or between you and your spouse? If so, to help you heal your hurting heart, please follow Don and Barb's example and seek help from a pastor or a biblical counselor.

## ASK YOURSELF

Have you come to realize that the well-being of your child rests securely in the hand of the One who created your son or daughter for

His glory and His purpose? If you have suffered a grievous loss, has this story given you hope that God can use it for good (Genesis 50:20)?

Consider that God is the one who molds each of our children in the womb, and He is the one who ordains the number of their days. Listen to what the psalmist said: "In thy book they were all written, even the days that were ordained for me, when as yet there was none of them" (Psalm 139:16 asv).

How might knowing God assigns a number of days to each person at conception help you trust Him more?

## 12

# Addicted to Each Other

### Jeff and Jennifer

Jeff and Jennifer are the first to admit their love story did not start out like a fairy tale. Jennifer said, "Our story is not what young girls hope for, and definitely not one I look forward to one day sharing with our children."

As a young adult Jennifer battled with feelings of being used or unwanted. She was determined to find a husband who would make her feel wanted for who she truly was, not just for what he could get from her. She was convinced her happiness would lie in marrying the right man.

For most of Jeff's life, he wrestled with feelings of inadequacy and loneliness. He had married when he was young, but that marriage ended in divorce, which added to his instability. He looked for relief in alcohol, and making one bad choice after another only contributed to his sense of hopelessness.

## THE COLLISION

"We were each masking our pain with people, places, and things," Jennifer said. "None of which ever led us to any sense of peace or freedom from the bondage we both carried. We were both lost and seeking fulfillment in all the wrong places."

Of the day she and Jeff met she said, "Then one day we collided into each other. Whether we knew it or not, it was really a case of each of us looking to the other for salvation."

Both believed in God. Jeff had been raised Catholic, and his idea of God was someone who punished sin. As a young girl Jennifer had given her heart to Jesus and gone to church with her parents. However, her church attendance stopped shortly after her parents' divorce. "From my upbringing, I knew the life I had been living was not one that honored the Lord, but I couldn't figure out how to change it. Shame was a constant source of my destruction."

*"Shame was a constant source of my destruction."*

When they started dating and their fleshly desires took over, Jennifer was secretly living under conviction that they were living in sin, and Jeff struggled privately with his fear of punishment. "We were both trying to find peace," Jennifer said, "but now we were seeking to find it in each other. Both of us partied back then. I drank alcohol and partied to feel love and acceptance. When I thought I found those things in Jeff, I no longer needed to drink. Jeff, on the other hand, continued drinking."

As time went by, Jeff and Jennifer did begin to find their worth in each other. "The joy we felt...seemed unbreakable," Jennifer said.

After three years of a whirlwind of both good and often bad choices, Jeff and Jennifer found themselves standing at the altar, pledging to love each other for the rest of their lives.

Jennifer recalled, "We had no understanding of the meaning of God's selfless love. We just wanted the other to fulfill our deepest needs."

## ADDICTED TO LOVE

Both Jeff and Jennifer continued to attempt to feed their insecurities through their addictions. Jennifer remembers, "Jeff had an addiction to substance and I had an addiction to codependency. We were addicted to each other."

Once Jennifer felt secure in Jeff's love for her, she no longer relied on drinking or partying to make her feel happy. But Jeff had no intention of stopping.

Jennifer thought, *I feel happiness with him, so I don't need to drink. If he is finding happiness in me, he shouldn't need to drink either.*

Jennifer said, "At this point in my life, I couldn't comprehend what real love was. To me, the longing to be loved had to be filled by a person. And my self-worth was wrapped up in how that person treated me."

As Jennifer continued to look to Jeff for her value, he pulled away from her. In desperation, she developed a habit of crying, manipulating, and even begging him to change. But when she told Jeff, "If you really loved me you would stop drinking," he drank even more.

The more expectations Jennifer laid on Jeff, the more miserably he failed. It soon became apparent to her that Jeff's drinking was truly an addiction—a coping mechanism and a way of life. But she had no idea how to help him.

All the while, their love for each other was deep, even in their seasons of struggle. Jennifer said, "There has never been a dull moment in this adventure we chose to take together, always filled with lots of laughter, tremendous passion, and strong commitment."

But Jennifer was confused about why their undying love couldn't fix their desperate situation. She cried to God for help. *Why is this happening to me?* But she admits that her asking God for help had nothing to do with wanting true help from what a relationship with Christ could offer. Her prayers were more like rubbing a magic lamp, hoping her wish for the craziness to go away would be granted.

*Jennifer was confused about why their undying love couldn't fix their desperate situation.*

## MAYBE WE SHOULD TRY CHURCH

Over the next three years Jeff's drinking was the source of most of the couple's tension and conflict. For Jennifer's sake Jeff tried desperately to quit drinking. But every time, fueled by guilt, he ended up going back to the bottle.

Occasionally Jeff and Jennifer would attend church, which they believed was a huge accomplishment. They convinced themselves going to church occasionally was better than not going at all.

After a particularly long period when Jeff was sober, Jennifer began to feel it was time to add to their family. They already enjoyed the blessing of time with Jeff's daughter from his previous marriage, but Jennifer could think of no better way to add to their joy than to have a child together.

When Jennifer got pregnant she thought, *Life cannot get any better. I have a gorgeous husband who loves me, and now we're going to have a baby!*

However, it wasn't long before Jennifer had to battle her insecurities. She began to worry about her ability to raise a child who would feel safe and loved. And she worried that Jeff might start drinking again.

In light of her frailty, Jennifer determined she couldn't raise a child without the strong support of a faith community, and she determined to make church attendance a priority for their family. Little did she know this was the beginning of one of the hardest seasons of their lives.

## DISTANT AND DAZED

Shortly after becoming pregnant, Jennifer's fear was realized when Jeff began to drink again. But this time he seemed different. Even on the days when he didn't drink, he was extremely distant.

Jennifer's pregnancy progressed, but their marriage digressed. As they battled over Jeff's addiction, Jennifer grew bitter and angry, which made Jeff even more distant from her. Jeff wasn't sleeping, he was losing weight, and his mind seemed to be withering away. Jennifer's anger turned to fear. She had no idea how to help her husband, or how to help herself.

Then it dawned on Jennifer that Jeff was in far greater trouble than she had imagined. Jeff was in a full-blown battle, with not only alcohol, but with drugs too.

Jennifer remembers feeling a glimmer of hope when she realized drugs were making Jeff react as he had been. She felt it was easier to blame the substance for his behavior than to blame him.

Looking back, Jennifer realizes they were both in a dark place. In fact, they were under spiritual attack. The battle was far greater than their understanding. Still seeking contentment in all the wrong places, they had no idea the peace they were looking for would come in a relationship with the Lord.

## HOPE

The first glimmer of hope came when Jennifer gave birth to their beautiful baby girl. "Words cannot express the love I felt," she said. "I could look at our baby and all my pain seemed to melt away."

Jennifer's elation was short-lived as Jeff's drug habit became increasingly worse. With the responsibility of caring for a baby and wrestling with Jeff's addictions, Jennifer felt her strength begin to fade. One day she told Jeff she was leaving unless he went to a treatment facility.

Jennifer loved Jeff deeply and did not want to abandon him in his fragile state. She secretly hoped her ultimatum would cause him to choose her and their daughter over the drugs and alcohol. It seemed like an easy choice to Jennifer, but she had little experience in understanding the battle of addiction.

## A DIFFICULT DECISION

Although leaving Jeff was the hardest thing she had ever done, Jennifer moved out of their house, taking their six-month-old baby with her.

Jennifer knew leaving was the right thing to do. She needed to protect herself and her daughter, but she felt terribly torn and guilty for abandoning her husband. Her motivation was that Jeff would miss them so desperately he would get help to prove his love and win her back.

With a broken heart and filled with fear, Jennifer realized this was her first real step of faith. She had no power to change Jeff and had no idea how she was going to get through this time of separation.

Through it all Jennifer's love and commitment to Jeff endured. She could see the man she knew he could be. She'd made vows to him, and she meant them. She was committed to do whatever she could to mend their brokenness.

## WHY PRAY WHEN YOU CAN WORRY?

Jennifer was completely devastated when Jeff continued to get worse. She missed him terribly and was concerned for his well-being. Her mind was constantly consumed with worry and fear. She rarely prayed. If she did pray she went back to her typical idea of rubbing the magic lamp to make a wish for God to help her.

Friends told her she needed to give up on Jeff and leave him for good, but Jennifer was determined to wait for him to get better. She looked for answers from people she had met at church, and there she found words of encouragement and support to hope for the reconciliation of her marriage—and her family. "I am forever grateful for the people who lovingly nudged me to seek the Lord with my life and for the restoration of my marriage."

However, Jennifer found herself responding with resentment when people simply told her, "Trust God. He will provide."

She thought, *You have no idea what I'm going through. It's just not that easy, people! How can you keep telling me to simply trust God?"*

After much resistance, Jennifer decided to memorize Proverbs 3:5-6, the scripture everyone kept reciting to her. "Trust in the Lord with all your heart, and lean not on your own understanding; in all your ways acknowledge Him, and He shall direct your paths."

She recited this passage over and over again. She said it until she believed it!

While Jeff and Jennifer were separated, they continued to talk every day. She was careful to remind Jeff how much she loved him while establishing and maintaining boundaries in their relationship.

As Jennifer's surrender to Christ began to transform her life, she tried desperately to share with Jeff the hope she'd found. But while she was finding strength in the Lord, Jeff's life was crumbling around him. The constant drug abuse had damaged his ability to think logically. At his darkest point, Jeff found himself huddled in a closet in his home, engulfed in thoughts of loneliness and despair.

## AND THEN...

In that moment when there seemed to be no hope for Jeff, he heard a knock at his front door. Remarkably, he pulled himself out of his closet to answer the door.

And even more remarkably, the man who knocked had come to share the gospel. He vaguely knew Jeff from work, and when he learned of his plight, he didn't hesitate to go to Jeff's home to share the gospel with him.

As the man explained how much Jesus loved him—so much so that He came to take the punishment for his sins and give him new life—God lifted the fog of Jeff's drug-induced stupor and gave him the ability to comprehend what the man was saying.

When the man told Jeff he could truly break free from the bondage holding him captive if he would only surrender his life to Jesus as His Lord and Savior, Jeff suddenly believed!

"In that moment God gave me clarity to understand and accept the message of the gospel. That day, on our front porch, I gave my life to the Lord."

When Jeff called Jennifer to share the news of his conversion, she could hardly believe her ears. God had answered her prayer in an amazing way! Within a week Jennifer had moved home and Jeff admitted himself to a treatment facility.

Jennifer recalled, "My husband's commitment in seeking restoration and healing was one of the most inspirational things I have ever witnessed."

Jeff and Jennifer began to regularly attend church and grew in their faith. Studying God's Word helped them realize their propensity to look to each other for the security only He can offer.

As Jeff worked at his rehabilitation, Jennifer discovered how her own feelings of need, resentment, and fear had contributed to their marriage trouble. As she studied Scripture her mind began to transform, and she discovered the peace of God. She had searched for it her whole life.

And when they thought their life could not be better, God blessed them with another baby girl. They soon realized that putting the Lord in the center of their relationship was the true answer they'd been missing. As their love grew in the Lord, their love grew for each other. Their spiritual journey together had truly begun.

The charm of Jeff and Jennifer's love story is how true love begins in loving God. Twenty years later, Jennifer says they are still learning and growing. And they are happy to share with others how true redemption is found in the ultimate love story of a relationship with Jesus.

## PONDER THIS

This story of Jeff and Jennifer's journey just blows me away. As you read their story, did you pick up on the base of their struggle? They were deeply in love, yet their love was not enough to fill the void in their hearts. Jennifer looked to Jeff to make her feel loved and Jeff looked to alcohol. Maybe you can identify with their story. Or maybe you know others in a similar circumstance.

*Jeff and Jennifer were deeply in love, yet their love was not enough to fill the void in their hearts. Consider the hope Jesus offers to anyone in a hopeless situation. God in His mercy allows people to make a mess of their lives to bring them to the end of themselves, so they will surrender to a relationship with Him. Realize that rescuing someone from their mess may not be the best way to help them. Sharing the gospel of salvation with them will.*

## ASK YOURSELF

While Jennifer acted in wisdom to separate herself from Jeff, she never gave up on him. Do you know a nonbeliever being held captive by an addiction? Let Jeff's story stir in you a new commitment to pray for their salvation.

Do you look to a person to make you feel valued? Learn from Jennifer's story and let today be the day you turn to Jesus as the One who will give you true worth and peace.

The Creator of the universe woos you to Himself so He can show you how much He loves you and longs to have a relationship with you. Consider the words of Jeremiah 31:3: "Yea, I have loved thee with an everlasting love: therefore with lovingkindness have I drawn thee" (KJV).

If you have never turned from your sin to a relationship with Jesus, let today be the day you humble yourself and cry out to Him for salvation.[1]

# 13

## The Perfect Husband

### Josh and Julie

As most young girls do, Julie often dreamed of the man she would marry one day and the beautiful wedding she planned to have. Along with adding to her growing list of wedding ideas, when she was twelve years old she also began making a list of traits she wanted in a husband. Of course, she wanted him to be handsome and romantic, but even at her young age she knew his most important quality would be his love for Christ.

Julie grew up in a Christian home in Atlanta, Georgia, where everyone agreed she was a "good girl." When other girls were dating, she showed little interest in relationships with boys. She recalled, "I was a good girl. In youth group I had signed a True Love Waits commitment card, and I showed my resolve to save myself for marriage by wearing a promise ring on the finger I hoped would one day wear a wedding ring."

Julie wasn't attracted to any of the boys in her life, so, she told me, "It was easy to be strong and remain sexually pure when there was no temptation."

After high school Julie landed an internship with a music production ministry in Texas. She was elated about the opportunity to work with the ministry and with the idea of an adventure that would take her to another state.

Once in Texas, she quickly learned about all the hard behind-the-scenes work that went into such a ministry. Rather than basking in the glamour of being involved in it, Julie found herself helping set up production in a hot, old warehouse in Tyler, Texas.

"I was sitting at a computer when some young guy named Josh walks up to me with a broom and tells me to sweep the warehouse floor. I didn't know who he was or why he had asked me to do so, but I agreed that the warehouse was dirty and started to sweep."

## YOU'RE BETTER THAN THAT

Josh grew up the oldest of ten children. His mother had home-schooled all of them through high school, so he had spent a lot of time studying independently while his mother saw to the education of his younger siblings.

From his unique upbringing, Josh learned the value of self-discipline and how to be self-motivated. And since he was smart and could finish his academic assignments rather quickly, he found a lot of time to explore his interest in sound design, learning to work the soundboard for his church and taking advantage of other production opportunities.

Once Josh graduated from high school, he was confident he wanted to pursue a career in sound and production. He was elated when he eventually landed a job with a production company in Tyler, Texas. But he had a young face, so even though he was older than he appeared and had a lot of experience in his field, gaining respect from interns wasn't going to be easy for him.

When Josh handed Julie the broom, little did she know she was the fifth person he had asked to sweep the warehouse—and that she was the only person who complied.

Later that day, when Julie's team was gathered for a meeting, Josh was introduced as their new manager. Julie thought, *Man, I'm glad I swept that floor. Who knew this guy was a member of the staff?*

Over the next several months, Josh and Julie became good friends as they worked together on their production. Julie recalled, "I found myself hoping to see Josh before or after every show. I remember how my heart would flutter with excitement every time Josh walked into the room—hoping he would notice me."

Julie's excitement turned to disappointment when she learned Josh had feelings for another girl. However, she resolved to continue to be Josh's friend. She was also aware of the company's strict policy against staff and interns dating, so technically she was in a better position to just enjoy Josh as a friend.

One day Josh kissed the other girl. Although she had allowed him to do it, she later reported the kiss to his bosses, and he was let go from his position. Staff dating interns was grounds for immediate dismissal. Although Josh explained he was unaware of the policy, he still suffered the consequences of his actions.

After Josh gathered his belongings, he went to find Julie to explain his departure. Julie recalled, "I remember Josh finding me on campus and telling me he had to leave. When he told me he had kissed the girl and that's why he was fired, my heart broke, and then I became infuriated with him.

"But then God lit a fire inside me to speak. I slammed my fist down on the table as I rose up out of my chair, proclaiming loudly, 'Josh Berry, you are so much better than that. God has big plans for your life. Stop being so stupid!'"

Josh knew Julie was right. Her courage to call him on his immature actions was exactly what he needed to hear. And those words were what triggered in Josh a deep admiration for Julie's passion for living a life surrendered to Christ.

They were silent as Julie drove Josh to the airport to fly back to his home in Nashville. She wondered if she would ever see him again, and he wondered what his next career steps should be. He also quietly considered the powerful statement Julie had made earlier when she said, "Josh, God has big plans for your life."

He hoped Julie was right. He was encouraged and inspired by the faith she had in the man he could become. Now he would need to live up to that expectation.

## I WANNA GROW OLD WITH YOU

Julie and Josh kept in touch through email. At first their emails were friendly updates of what each was doing from time to time. But as their friendship grew through their correspondence, so did their affection for each other.

*Josh was encouraged and inspired by the faith
Julie had in the man he could become.*

After months of emailing and occasional phone calls, Josh told Julie he had feelings for her, and Julie admitted she had fallen for him. As their friendship grew into a long-distance romance, every day Julie could hardly wait to see if Josh had written her another email. She longed to hear her computer say, "You've got mail." After she carefully pored over each word in the email, Julie would reread it several times to bask in Josh's sweet words.

Julie remembers, "These were fun times. And all I could think about every day was Josh. And getting an email from him was daily what I longed for."

When Julie completed her internship with the production company, she moved back home to live with her parents in Georgia. Soon Josh and Julie were taking turns driving back and forth between Nashville and Atlanta to see each other. Josh's romantic, thoughtful gestures served to capture Julie's heart.

On one of Julie's visits to Nashville, Josh led her to an old oak tree in his backyard, where he had hung a double swing—just for her. As the two sat enjoying the sway of the swing, Josh leaned over to kiss Julie. She told me, "My heart skipped a beat. This was our first kiss—and not only that, it was *my* first kiss ever! Josh is my first love. That kiss was everything!"

Instantly Julie knew Josh was the one she hoped for so many years ago when she made the list for the type of man she wanted to marry. From then on Julie's mind was captivated by thoughts of marriage to Josh, and she secretly began planning the wedding of her dreams.

"Josh is definitely a man with a plan," Julie shared. So while she was privately planning their dream wedding, Josh was secretly plotting the romantic way he would ask Julie to be his bride.

On the day he proposed, he invited Julie to come with him to the church where he had just been hired to work as a sound and media technician. While the two were seated on the front pew in the auditorium, the song "I Wanna Grow Old with You" began to play over the sound system.

When Julie heard the lyrics, she turned to look into Josh's eyes. When his gaze met hers, a smile came across his face. Josh quietly asked, "Will you marry me?" He squeezed her left hand gently into his.

"Yes!" Julie said, laughing joyfully. She then jokingly added, "But you have to kneel down and give me a ring."

Immediately Josh was down on one knee, and then lifting her hand so she could see it, he showed Julie that she was already wearing the engagement ring!

"How'd you do that?" Julie said, squealing.

Early on in their dating relationship, Josh usually held Julie by her left hand, and while he held her hand he developed a habit of moving her purity ring on and off her ring finger. Julie said, "I got so used to that funny little habit that the day he proposed I was oblivious that he had switched my promise ring with an engagement ring."

Julie recalled, "Josh blew my mind with his thoughtfulness and attention to every romantic detail."

But Julie was even more amazed when Josh explained to her how from the time he knew she was "the one" he had started playing with the promise ring on her left hand's ring finger, knowing one day he would surprise her with an engagement ring in the manner he just had.

## EVERYTHING WAS PERFECT...

Once the couple was engaged, they began planning the wedding Julie had always hoped for. The idea of their long-distance relationship finally being over and the two of them never having to say good-bye again was something they both longed for.

Whenever Josh and Julie made the long drive to be together during their engagement, they thought it would be all right to spend more and more time alone as a couple. Knowing they would soon be married, the two began to go physically farther than they had ever intended before their wedding day. And one day Julie faced the painful realization that she had become pregnant with Josh's baby.

Josh and Julie's parents did their best to support them when they learned of the unexpected pregnancy. Julie's heart was broken when she agreed to change their wedding plans from her lifelong dream wedding to a rushed ceremony in a little country church. Julie recalled, "All the stress of a shotgun wedding, and all the disappointment we had caused our families put an unbelievable strain on me mentally, emotionally, and physically."

Six weeks later Julie miscarried their baby. The doctor could give them no clear reason why they lost the child, but Julie believed it was because of all the stress she'd been under in the early months of pregnancy.

## THE FIRST YEAR

Their first year of marriage was difficult. Julie remembers, "We struggled to find our identities. We had to learn how to forgive each other for surrendering to our passions before marriage, and we needed to accept God's forgiveness for ourselves."

They didn't want to pretend everything was all right at home, so they reached out for help by confiding in close friends for support and counsel. And they plugged into a church where they would hear teaching from God's Word and develop relationships with other believers who would encourage them as well.

Julie said, "Our families prayed for us, and we surrendered ourselves and our marriage to the Lord. We held on to Christ and we clung to each other. Through our struggle we learned so much about ourselves and each other."

Things settled as the couple began making loving Christ their life's priority. Soon they decided it was time to move to Nashville, where

Josh had lived for many years before they wed. He had business contacts, friends, and a good community of support in Nashville, so he and Julie were certain moving there was a good idea for their family.

Life was good for them in Nashville—it became their home. Soon the couple bought their first house, and God blessed them with two sons, Conrad and Emmitt.

"Living the dream life" is how Josh and Julie described those early years. The couple had learned to love and support each other, and raising two sons together seemed to make their life complete.

God blessed Josh's career in the Christian music industry. Traveling with well-known music artists and launching a production company that produced their shows was a wonderful way for him to use his talent for the kingdom of God. Julie was incredibly proud of her husband, and she prayed for him as he worked to keep Christ and his family his primary focus amid an extremely busy schedule on the road.

Josh wisely sought counsel from pastors and others in ministry who had raised their families well during the pull of career. Balancing his passion for his profession and his adoration for his family was something Josh was committed to achieve.

## AN UNEXPECTED ADVENTURE

"We were right in the thick of kindergarten and potty training when life threw us an unexpected adventure," Julie said.

When she began having episodes where her entire left side would go numb and seize up, she knew something was wrong. After one serious episode, when she could ignore her symptoms no longer, Josh drove her to the hospital. All the way there Julie imagined the worst possible diagnosis for her progressing condition.

After she underwent a series of tests, the doctor delivered Julie's diagnosis. "You have multiple sclerosis."

Julie was surprised how relieved she was when she heard the news. She had been so concerned that the tests would reveal a life-threatening condition, that MS somehow seemed a manageable diagnosis for her mind to process.

Josh, on the other hand, felt helpless. All he wanted to do was figure out a way to fix the problem. He immediately began to research multiple sclerosis and possible medications to help Julie's condition. He set up appointments for Julie with some of the leading experts in MS and drove her to meet with the specialists. Josh was deflated when they learned the medication suggested by the doctors would cost an exorbitant amount they couldn't possibly afford.

Still trying to fix Julie's problem, Josh researched holistic methods to treat her MS. For a while Julie went along with Josh's quest to find answers for her ailment, but finally she came to the point where she said, "Josh, I am so thankful for all your effort to help, but I just need God to show us what He wants us to do."

Enlisting the prayer support of Christian friends all over the country, Julie waited for God to show her the way He would have her go. "I prayed for a big neon sign. That sign came in the form of a phone number given to me, of a person who had been living with MS for a very long time. I was nervous to call the number because I didn't know the person. But one day while my baby was sleeping, I asked God to give me the courage to make the call. I picked up the phone and dialed the number."

The man on the other end of the phone was kind, compassionate, and full of wisdom for Julie's plight. "After a 45-minute conversation, I hung up feeling encouraged. This man who had lived with MS provided the wisdom I had been praying for all along."

The man had encouraged Julie to never give up hope and to fight back against the disease threatening to debilitate her. His words rang in her ears: "What the Enemy means to use to destroy us is the very thing that will give God glory. We must choose every day to let the joy of the Lord be our strength."

With new insight and passion for life, Julie began to adjust her mind to rejoice amid her trial, and God truly became her source of strength. Her unexpected health issues have caused Josh and Julie to be grateful for the good days and fight for joy on the days she struggles. Julie's fragile state has certainly caused the couple to keep their eyes on Jesus. And Julie's frailty has taught her to rely on prayer support and help from friends as well.

*"What the Enemy means to use to destroy us
is the very thing that will give God glory."*

Today Julie is in remission and praises God for every day she wakes up feeling well. She says, "Circumstances change us. Life changes us. And thank God He continues to shape us, and it's wonderful!"

## PONDER THIS

As a young girl Julie made a commitment to save sex for marriage. Keeping her commitment seemed easy when there was no real temptation. Once she and Josh fell in love and became engaged, however, their resolve to wait to have sex until they were married was challenged. If you're not yet married, or you're in a serious relationship, you may think you would never fall to such temptation. Like Julie, you might be tempted to think, *I'm a good girl. I'm confident I will remain sexually pure for marriage.*

Not long ago I spoke on sexual purity at a women's chapel for a Christian college. I shared with the young women how the things many of them may be doing with their boyfriends were the very acts God ordained only for husbands and wives to enjoy a wonderful sexual experience. I warned those who were toying with their sexual passions that believing they could restrain themselves from having sex before marriage was naive and a deception from the Enemy. The Bible warns that Satan looks for ways to take advantage of anyone who is ignorant of his devices (2 Corinthians 2:11).

I was surprised by two very different responses from the young women. Most thanked me for being so real and calling them on their sin. But another group of women said my talk offended them as they would *never* involve themselves in such unspiritual actions.

First Corinthians 10:12 warns, "Let him who thinks he stands take heed lest he fall" (KJV). In over thirty years of ministry, I have sat across from young women who had the same confidence in their ability to abstain from sex before marriage, only to have fallen to the temptation once they fell in love. Rather than putting your faith in your own ability to refrain from sex after you fall in love, you would be wise to realize you just might find yourself surrendering to your passions if you don't daily abide in Christ and ask Him for help to remain pure.

## ASK YOURSELF

As with all marriages, Josh and Julie have faced some ups and downs. Notice how throughout their story you find them looking to older, wiser, godly people to walk them through their struggles.

When you face trials in your marriage, are you tempted to hide your problems for fear of what others will think of you? Learn from Josh and Julie's example. Make yourself vulnerable to some trusted Christian friends, family, or pastors who will stand with you in steadfast prayer and guide you through your trials with a biblical perspective.

Christ, your marriage, and godly counselors form a powerful cord that cannot be quickly broken (Ecclesiastes 4:12).

## 14

*Surprised by Love*

### Matt and Becca

Becca stood in front of her bedroom mirror, sighed, and threw another outfit on her bed. The pile of discarded clothes was growing bigger. A friend had invited her to a Christmas party that evening, and none of the outfits she'd tried seemed right. This one was too flirty, that one too dressy. Finally, she pulled on a pair of jeans and a casual top. This party wasn't about finding a date.

Becca was a thirtysomething single mom living in Seattle. She was devoted to her daughter and to her work as a social worker, where she found satisfaction in helping others work through difficult issues of life. That night she decided to attend a Christmas party, the last thing she was looking for was a husband.

Matt, who had once been a radio host in the Seattle area, had taken a job as a digital content manager for KLove, a popular Christian radio station in California. Matt no longer lived in Seattle, but each year his friends looked forward to his return there to visit his parents and host his annual Christmas party at their house.

Matt recalled, "Before I flew out to Seattle, I remember distinctly, I didn't bring any nice clothes with me because I didn't want to meet anyone while I was there. I was not looking for a long-distance relationship."

Becca laughed as she added, "I went to the party strictly to have fun—but no dating. I didn't even dress up."

So there they were, two young adults set on having a fun time at a Christmas party, but so intent on not meeting anyone there to date that each underdressed for the occasion.

## JUST A POOR RADIO GUY

At the party Becca was enjoying a cup of coffee at the coffee bar. After putting the final touches on decorations for the event, Matt walked over there to order his favorite drink from the barista.

Becca noticed Matt, but she was unimpressed. She thought he was "a snobby guy who worked for a radio station in California."

When Matt struck up a conversation with her, she tried hard not to, but she couldn't help but like the guy. "He seemed sweet, and he was easy to talk to." And she liked that Matt didn't take himself too seriously.

While Becca listened to Matt talk about the details of his life, she realized how she had misjudged him. She thought, *He's just a poor, down-to-earth radio guy.*

## DON'T OVERLOOK A SINGLE MOM

As Matt listened to Becca, he couldn't help but be drawn to her gentleness. Even when she told Matt she had a daughter, he didn't shy away. Growing up in church, he had been told not to overlook single mothers, but to value them.

After an enjoyable evening of getting to know each other, both Matt and Becca had forgotten about their commitment to not date anyone they met at the party. They exchanged phone numbers and parted ways.

The next day Matt and Becca were texting back and forth. At one point Becca's phone lit up. She assumed it was a text from Matt and grabbed the phone right away. But it was a notification from a dating site where she had added her profile before ever meeting Matt. To Becca's surprise, the dating site had notified her of a possible match. Becca said, "And there it was, Matt's face on my phone!"

Becca was more than intrigued. Not only had she been thinking about Matt nonstop, but now a dating site had pinged her phone because he just might be the one for her. When Matt asked Becca out on their first date, she readily accepted his invitation.

## SURPRISED BY LOVE

Matt and Becca went out to dinner and talked for four hours. Afterward they toured Seattle's downtown to look at Christmas lights. Not wanting the evening to end, the two settled on a park bench. Becca recalled that, as they talked into the night, "We felt like we had been together forever."

And then Matt asked if he could kiss her. By the end of their first date Becca knew she was going to love Matt forever.

Matt said, "I knew that one day God would just surprise me with the one I would love." Meeting Becca was certainly a surprise.

As Matt and Becca continued to learn more about each other, Matt discovered how much Becca's faith in Christ influenced all aspects of her life. "When she asked me 'Do you read your Bible daily?' and 'Who are you praying for today?' I knew she had a deep faith in God." And that was exactly what Matt wanted in a wife.

Right from the beginning Becca was determined to find out about Matt's relationship with the Lord. "I was in my thirties, and I knew what things were important to me. And I needed to know if Matt had the qualities that would fulfill them."

Matt had Christmas dinner with Becca and her family. While they were playing games after dinner, Becca noticed the instant connection her daughter, Reeci, seemed to have with Matt. Becca knew she not only had to consider him a possible husband, but also a potential father for her little girl. Becca thought, *Wow, he would make a great dad for her. This guy is special.*

Matt also understood the importance of his role in Reeci's life, should he and Becca move forward in their relationship. Matt could see how much Reeci wanted a daddy by how she responded to his attention.

After the holidays Matt had to return to his job in California. Before he left, Becca told Matt she loved him. At that point Matt didn't respond with an "I love you too." However, three weeks later, when

Becca went to see him in California, he was more than ready to tell her he loved her.

Matt courted Becca over the long distance. Through phone calls, FaceTime, and social media, the two fell deeply in love. And Reeci was always right in the middle of it. Matt said, "Even when we were dating and FaceTiming, she would say, 'You're my mommy and you're my daddy' and then run away and laugh." Matt realized Reeci was testing the waters because she really wanted him to be her dad.

Becca recalled, "Matt did a lot to win her over. He sent her postcards. Even when Matt proposed he gave her a separate gift. It was a little box and necklace. Matt treated her so special. I appreciated that."

## WHEN GOD IS THE MATCHMAKER

When Matt asked Becca to marry him, she had no doubt that she wanted to spend the rest of her life with him. "I felt like God matched us up. I had a peace, and I knew God was orchestrating everything."

Becca didn't hesitate to say yes when Matt asked her to be his wife, even though it would mean leaving family and friends in Seattle. Leaving would be hard, but Becca was ready for this new great adventure God had given them.

Matt continues to work for Christian radio. Not long after they were married, he and Becca began a ministry the two of them could do together. Because they're passionate about helping build strong marriages centered on God's grace, they started a podcast called *Engaging Story*.[1] On the program Matt and Becca interview couples with strong marriages. By inviting couples to share their love stories, they're encouraging others to honor their marriage covenant while offering hope to struggling couples who may be feeling isolated and alone.

## PONDER THIS

Isn't it fun to hear stories about how God surprises people with love? Watching God play matchmaker is certainly one of my favorite things about mentoring young women.

*All too often women get so swept up in the excitement of a new relationship that they don't take time to inquire into the spiritual maturity of the man.*

Becca was a single mom who wasn't desperate to find a man. Rather, she had come to terms with the type of husband and father she was looking for. She asked probing questions at the onset of her relationship with Matt. All too often women get so swept up in the excitement of a new relationship that they don't take time to inquire into the spiritual maturity of the man.

If you're single, learn from Becca's story and have the courage to find out if a man truly loves Jesus. The sooner you discover the depth of his faith, or lack thereof, the easier it will be to withdraw your attentions—before your heart becomes so involved that you overlook any red flags.

## ASK YOURSELF

Do you think it's harder for a woman to be lonely while she waits for God to bring to her a godly man, or harder for a godly woman who marries an ungodly man to be lonely in her marriage?

In my experience as a pastor's wife, I can attest to the loneliness a Christian woman experiences when she marries a man who doesn't share her love for Christ. Single women who know Jesus and choose to ignore His instruction to marry a Christ follower often struggle with loneliness and regret after they're married.

Single women, let God write your love story. Ask Him to grant you His wisdom to discern the heart of any man who catches your attention. And have the courage to ask probing questions about his faith. (If you are a married woman, consider coming alongside a single woman to teach her this valuable lesson.)

*Single women, let God write your love story. Ask Him to grant you His wisdom to discern the heart of any man who catches your attention.*

Consider this insight from the apostle Paul in Ephesians 5:3-10 (ESV):

> But sexual immorality and all impurity or covetousness must not even be named among you, as is proper among saints. Let there be no filthiness nor foolish talk nor crude joking, which are out of place, but instead let there be thanksgiving. For you may be sure of this, that everyone who is sexually immoral or impure, or who is covetous (that is, an idolater), has no inheritance in the kingdom of Christ and God. Let no one deceive you with empty words, for because of these things the wrath of God comes upon the sons of disobedience. Therefore do not become partners with them; for at one time you were darkness, but now you are light in the Lord. Walk as children of light (for the fruit of light is found in all that is good and right and true), and try to discern what is pleasing to the Lord.

# 15

## Connected at the Heart

### Bill and Pam

Pam grew up with an alcoholic father. With his drinking came bouts of rage that resulted in domestic violence. The abuse Pam experienced at the hand of her father burned deeply into her subconscious as the voice in her head continually whispered, "You are unworthy, unlovable, unwanted, and unbecoming."

Pam became her own worst critic. Surely, she reasoned, her father would love her if she weren't so imperfect. But when Pam turned eight years old, her life was changed forever when the insecure little girl from a chaotic home learned of Jesus's love for her. As she came to realize He was the only one who could heal her hurting heart and brokenness, she made the best decision of her life in surrendering to Him as her Lord and Savior.

Pam was delighted when only a few months later her mother came to know Jesus as well. As she and her mother grew in their faith over the years, her father became more and more angry and abusive. His fits of rage became so intense that her mother feared he might one day kill one of them, himself—or both. Finally she found the courage to remove herself and her children from the nightmare they'd been living.

## FEARFUL OR FEARLESS?

Bill was raised by a mother who struggled with emotional and mental health issues because of trauma she'd experienced. Living under the shadow of her fear was the foundation of his upbringing. His mother was so overwhelmed by even the smallest details of life that Bill began to grocery shop, cook, and do laundry for himself at the age of nine.

When he was a teenager, the pendulum of fear would swing to the opposite extreme for Bill, who was determined to be courageous. His fearlessness even landed him the coveted high school quarterback position. Bill's commitment to bravery, however, wavered one night when he went with some friends to see a horror film. The movie triggered a fear in his heart that sent him looking for answers in the Bible. When he read "Greater is he that is in you, than he that is in the world" (1 John 4:4 KJV), he realized the true path to living without fear was in a surrender to Jesus as his Lord and Savior. Bill gave his heart to Christ, and he began a life where he learned how to be set free from any fear that held him back from becoming the man God called him to be.

God often uses the pain in our lives for His kingdom purposes. As a young boy Bill couldn't have imagined that the influence of his mother's fearful tendencies and his parents' tenuous relationship would be what God would use to prepare him for his future.

*God often uses the pain in our lives for His kingdom purposes.*

By the time Bill graduated high school, he was convinced God was calling him into ministry. With the Lord's courage to guide him, he enrolled in a Christian college.

At the same time, Pam had a deep yearning to equip herself to become a woman God could use in her generation, and she was convinced attending a Bible college was the right choice.

Although Bill and Pam attended different schools, their paths crossed at a Campus Crusade leadership conference where they each committed their lives to full-time Christian work.

## GOD CONNECTED THEIR HEARTS

At the conference Bill entered the lobby through one door and sat down on a sofa. Pam entered the lobby through a different door and casually seated herself on the couch across from Bill. When Bill noticed the beautiful girl, he fearlessly decided to break the ice. "What did God teach you today?"

As Pam began to share all she had been learning at the conference and her heart's desire to serve the Lord, Bill was even more drawn to her inner beauty. And when he divulged what God was teaching him and how he also had surrendered to serve Christ in full-time ministry, Pam was captivated by him. "On that day God connected our hearts," she told me.

As a young girl, Pam's criteria for finding a husband had been "I don't want to marry an angry alcoholic like my father." But after growing in her walk with Christ, her focus had become not on what type of man she *didn't* want, but rather on wanting a husband who was just like her heavenly Father. Bill seemed to be that type of man.

By the end of the conference, Bill and Pam knew they wanted to pursue a relationship. When Bill pulled out a spiral notebook with a list of relationship-guiding questions, Pam knew she had found a man who had the same heart she did, wishing to date in a manner that would honor Christ. Honoring the Lord became the foundation of their relationship. As the two began their dating journey, Pam and Bill chose to base their relationship on 1 Samuel 2:30: "Those who honor me I will honor" (ESV).

And honor Him they did. So much so that Pam and Bill decided their dating life would not be centered on any physical interaction. They were so determined to honor God with purity in their relationship that they agreed to not even kiss until they were engaged—should God lead them to marry.

Because their dating life was not caught up in physical intimacy, Bill and Pam spent many hours talking to one another—sharing their hopes and dreams while discussing all that God was teaching them in their biblical studies. And since they were both walking in purity before the Lord, they were being led by the Holy Spirit to discern God's plan for their relationship.

After nine months of dating, Bill and Pam were convinced they were in love. However, the two wanted God's direction before stepping into marriage, so they agreed to take a break for eight weeks over the summer. They agreed not to write, call, or see each other as they pressed into asking God to show them His will for their relationship.

As Bill waited and prayed, he worked hard cleaning swimming pools to save up money to buy an engagement ring for Pam—should God grant him his heart's desire to marry the woman he had fallen in love with so deeply.

Meanwhile Pam sought the Lord's direction as she studied diligently at Institute for Biblical Studies.

## GOD CONNECTED THEIR FUTURES

When the two reunited at the end of the summer, they were both confident God was calling them to be together, not only as husband and wife but also in ministry as fellow servants of Jesus. Pam said, "We both knew we would love to love each other for the rest of our lives!"

Shortly after, near a beach where Pam and Bill had often gone on dates, Bill knelt on one knee and sang a song to Pam he had written just for her. Then ever so sweetly he said, "God has brought us together. Will you marry me? Will you kiss me for the first time?"

In excited enthusiasm Pam joyfully exclaimed, "Yes!"

## GOD CONNECTED THEIR
## SPIRITS—AND THEIR BODIES

Only four months after the engagement, Bill and Pam married in a lovely ceremony. They agreed marriage is the best decision a couple can make, and they were determined to live each day celebrating that decision.

To remind each other of the reason for their love, both Bill and Pam had 1 John 4:19 etched into the wedding gifts they gave each other: "We love because he first loved us" (ESV).

From their first kiss when they got engaged to their glorious first kiss as husband and wife, kissing became a common interaction between

Bill and Pam. One romantic practice they began when they got married has continued. Pam said, "In addition to our radical decision to wait until engagement to kiss, we have also made it a romantic ritual to kiss each other every time after we say grace. We have never missed a kiss in 37 years of marriage!"

The honeymoon did not disappoint. Bill and Pam agree waiting to have sex until marriage was undoubtedly one of the best decisions they could have made. As they learned to enjoy one another in the marriage bed, their foundational scripture, "Those who honor me I will honor" (1 Samuel 2:30 esv), certainly proved true as He blessed their sexual intimacy within the bounds of marriage.

Pam said, "When Bill and I first met, we decided we were going to do our best to love each other according to God's guidelines. Yes, some might think our decision to not have sex until marriage was old-fashioned, but those old-fashioned values—God's values—worked for us! And I am confident they will work for everyone who wants God's best for their love too."

While honoring God brought His blessing in Bill and Pam's union, coming together in marriage soon began to reveal the deep wounds each had endured in their upbringing. Pam shared this memory from their honeymoon.

"On our honeymoon, I stepped out of the shower, and I was looking in the mirror while blow-drying my hair and applying makeup. As I looked into the mirror, all the old messages began to play in my mind: unworthy, unlovable, unwanted, and unbecoming. So I began to criticize myself from head to toe out loud."

Bill was sitting on the bed and thought, *Oh dear! She's going to get all depressed, and it's going to take the rest of our honeymoon to pull her out of this negative spiral.* He prayed, *Lord, can you help a guy out here?*

Just then a thought crossed Bill's mind he knew was heaven sent. He thought, *Bill, you could do a better job than that mirror.*

Pam recalled, "Instead of getting angry at me, Bill came over to me and gently wrapped me in his strong arms. He took my face in his hands and looked deep into my eyes and said, 'Pam, let me be your mirror. If you need to know what a beautiful, godly, amazing woman you are—you come see me!' And then with a sweet smile Bill added, 'If I have to break every mirror in the house to get you to believe me, I will. But from this point on, let me be your mirror.'"

Immediately Pam's mood changed. "The outpouring of God's love through Bill revived my life, my hope, and my ability to receive and give love." Bill's kindness in ministering to Pam at the place of her vulnerability set a strong foundation for their love. And through Bill's example and ministry, God is now guiding countless husbands to respond in the same manner to their wives.

## GOD WHISPERED HIS LOVE
## INTO THEIR LOVE STORY

Living in community, and especially within marriage, is one way God helps us peel back some of the layers of pain we might have long since ignored. God loves us so much He sends people into our lives to move us out of our comfort zones to become more and more the image of Christ. God used the first five years of Pam and Bill's marriage to do just that.

> *Living in community, and especially within marriage,*
> *is one way God helps us peel back some of the*
> *layers of pain we might have long since ignored.*

Pam recalled, "We were two imperfect individuals that God was working to redeem. Me from the pain of being raised by an abusive alcoholic father, and Bill from the impact of a childhood dominated by fear and emotional brokenness. But God's love overcomes issues. God's love redeems and restores."

While working to finish their college degrees and ministering to their church's youth group, Bill and Pam experienced many financial struggles. Amid their trials, however, God showed them incredible things about Himself by meeting their needs in ways they never could have imagined. For example, after riding bicycles everywhere for an entire year, God surprised them when He answered the prayers of their youth group and blessed them with a car—an older model that had been driven by the grandparents of one of the kids. The values of family and community were woven even into this gift.

## GOD CONNECTED THEIR MINISTRIES

During those years while finishing their education, God gave Bill and Pam a deep love for helping people with their relationships.

After completing their bachelor degrees, Bill went on to earn his master of divinity degree. God called the couple to minister in San Diego, California, where at the young age of 28 Bill became a lead pastor. Immediately Bill and Pam went to work helping people with their relationships. Their goal was to help them love wisely, which eventually became the founding theme for their ministry, Love-Wise. And their pondering about how God made men and women different from creation on, eventually led them to write their bestselling book, *Men Are Like Waffles, Women Are Like Spaghetti.*

God blessed Bill and Pam with three amazing sons, which eventually stirred in them a desire to write books to help others raise their own children to follow Christ.

## GOD CONNECTED THEIR LEGACIES

That little spiral notebook Bill had packed with relationship questions eventually was published as *The Before-You-Marry Book of Questions,* which has helped singles and couples in love—including their own sons—learn to make wise relationship choices. Their sons have grown up to marry godly women and are now raising their own children. Pam knows God put in her heart the longing to be a woman of influence and that He has accomplished through her what He ordained before the foundations of this world (Ephesians 2:8-10). Bill has equipped men to be their wives' best friends while Pam has inspired women with *52 Ways to Wow Your Husband.* And together they help married couples embrace and enjoy God's gift of "red-hot monogamy" with a book by that title.

As two young adults, each carrying the wounds of a dysfunctional childhood, God brought Bill and Pam together for His kingdom purpose. Over the years their ministry has touched countless hearts and helped more marriages than they would have thought possible. Bill and Pam know they could not have made it this far in their marriage had it not been for their wholehearted devotion to honor Christ, and for the love of family and friends.

Down deep Pam and Bill know the verse they claimed on their wedding day, "We love because he first loved us" (1 John 4:19 ESV) is the only reason they can live happily ever after.

## PONDER THIS

It came as no surprise to God that Pam was raised by an alcoholic father with a terrible temper. And God knew Bill would be brought up by a mom who struggled. Both Pam and Bill grew up watching their parents' marriages that were anything but happy. Rather than allowing the familiarity of their upbringing to define the type of marriage they would pursue, Pam and Bill surrendered their hearts and their futures to Christ. And God used their painful upbringing to equip them to help others build healthy marriages founded in Jesus Christ.

It's easy to excuse our unhealthy relationship habits if we've been raised in dysfunction (and let's be honest, we are all sinners, so all of us have experienced dysfunction to some degree). But God has more for your relationship than what you may be tempted to accept as "normal."

Are you willing to let go of familiar but ungodly ways to instead seek God's plan for your relationship?[1]

## ASK YOURSELF

Consider the words of Pam and Bill's foundational scripture, "Those who honor me I will honor" (1 Samuel 2:30 ESV). Would you say your marriage honors God? Or are you more concerned about receiving respect at any cost? What can you learn from Bill and Pam's story to help you make adjustments in your own marriage?

Do you wrestle with a self-defeating voice in your head as the result of a painful childhood? Whether or not your husband kindly says, "Let me be your mirror," you can find your worth in allowing Jesus to be the reflection of His perfect love that will quench the wrong image you have of yourself.

If you're not married, are you willing to honor Christ in your relationships as you seek His will for your future? Learning to honor God above all else will result in a life well lived—with no regrets. Take some time to surrender to Christ the purity in your dating life, and ask Him to help you rise above what culture says is acceptable to honor His guidelines for your life and relationships.

If you have never surrendered to Jesus as your Lord and Savior, I pray today will be the day of salvation for you so that God can empower you to live the life He has planned for you—a life that rises above any dysfunction that may have scarred your life.

## 16

# A Chance Encounter

## James and Valder

In the fall of 1982, Valder found herself staring at a page of classified ads while drinking her morning coffee and wondering how she'd come to this point. Her marriage had failed, the divorce was final, and she somehow had to find a way to provide for her two young sons. Looking for work to provide for her family had become her top priority.

Valder came across a magazine article that boasted of abundant job opportunities in Dallas, Texas. Looking back, she remembers how the article caught her eye, gave her hope, and motivated her to uproot her little family to settle there.

Courageously, Valder packed up her belongings, and she and her sons relocated to Texas—even before she'd found work in Dallas. Fortunately, the magazine article had not exaggerated about the availability of jobs there. Within a month Valder had been hired as a department supervisor in her field of technology.

With her new income Valder was able to rent a wonderful home for her family in East Dallas. She remembers, "The neighborhood I lived in was a lot like living in Europe—I had lived there while being raised by my military parents. The community had small stores within walking distance, and walking and bike riding were the modes of transportation."

Valder was happy in her new life. She was doing well in her career, and her children had adjusted nicely to the transition.

After a year in Dallas, while walking to the store one day, Valder happened upon an attractive man named James. As she smiled and James introduced himself, there seemed to be an immediate connection between the two.

Valder was happy when James accompanied her on the rest of her walk to the store. She learned James and his brother, Joseph, were from Michigan. Both were iron workers, and the two had come to Dallas in search of temporary work because Michigan's auto industry had started to decline.

## AN ORDINARY DAY

Valder could hardly believe how her everyday life had been interrupted by meeting such an amazing man. Who would have thought God would bring such a wonderful encounter into an otherwise ordinary day?

To Valder's delight, James asked to see her again. For the next two weeks they spent every spare moment with each other. In that short time they each began to think they were falling in love.

Sadly, their newfound romance was interrupted when at the end of those two weeks James had to return to Michigan. Valder remembers both of them attempting not to make too big a deal of his departure. "It was an unceremonious parting on both our parts."

Since Valder and James had been dating for only two weeks, saying good-bye should not have been so difficult—but it was. They continued their budding romance through phone calls and letters.

As Valder learned more about James, she discovered he had once been a professional singer and a lead vocalist for his own band. If she hadn't thought he was amazing before, Valder soon discovered what a hopeless romantic James was when he called her one Saturday morning.

"Valder, I have a song for you." With that, he broke into singing the song made famous by Stevie Wonder, "I Just Called to Say I Love You." (Now that song is rolling around in your head, isn't it? Mine too!)

At the conclusion of James's song, he declared his love for her and said, "I can't live without you."

That was it. In that moment Valder was completely smitten with James. She recalled, "Oh, my heart melted, and I confessed to James that I could not imagine my life without him."

As James daily professed his love for Valder, she reciprocated his affections and began declaring her love for him in her letters. Valder remembers what a big step it was for her to do that.

James worked out a plan to relocate to Dallas so he could spend time with Valder. During their continued courtship the two grew deeply in love.

To show their family and friends how they had come to believe that God is the greatest source of true love, the couple chose to marry on Valentine's Day, in 1985. James, the romantic, wrote their wedding vows:

> I say these vows once and only once to thee. Be my love,
> my life, my Partner in Productivity. I take you to be my
> beloved, to love God, you and our family. To honor you,
> to treasure you, to be at your side in the good times, and
> in the bad, and to love and cherish you always. I promise
> you this from my heart and soul, for all the days of my life.

Along with learning to adjust to each other as newlyweds, James learned how to be a loving stepfather to Valder's two children.

Over time, God also blessed Valder and James with two more wonderful children. All their kids are now grown. Valder explained, "We love the power of love in our marriage journey. In our 31 years of marriage, James and I have fallen more in love with each passing year. We have faithfully held on to each other as the vicissitudes of life have impacted us."

Valder continued, "As we have taken on the adventures of life, we have stood on the foundation of our belief in God; raised four children; had…annual love celebrations (a community event that honors marriage); created our company, PIP Production; managed our individual careers; and shared our collective paths of success as husband and wife and a family."

Valder and James's high-profile marriage has been a profound role model in this generation. In 2005 they were awarded the Dallas

Marriage of the Year Award. And in 2007 the Beebes were inducted into the National Black Marriage Hall of Fame. Their union has been profiled as a role model marriage in several magazines as well. In a 2008 issue of *Essence* magazine, the Beebes gave God glory for their happy marriage when they said, "What is the key to our love and sustaining our love? We love the Lord God with all our heart and soul, and we love others around us, as we love ourselves."

Through Valder's radio program, *The Valder Beebe Show*, and various events, the Beebes are committed to help all the marriages they can. When I appeared as a guest on Valder's radio program, I asked her about their love story. She passionately proclaimed, "We love to tell people about our love story. And we want to help everyone who desires to have a chance to experience the joy we have."

Over three decades ago a single mom ventured to Dallas to find work. At the same time, a handsome iron worker took a short detour to Dallas—also in search of work. While both were looking for a better life in Texas, neither could have imagined what God had in store for them on the day they met. But God knew. Valder and James's profound love for God has been the key to their happiness in marriage. And now it's their passion to help other married couples discover this profound secret to happiness as well.

## PONDER THIS

God used a lack of work to bring both Valder and James to cross paths in Dallas, Texas. Let that sit with you for a moment. Learning God's ways as He reveals His attributes through the pages of Scripture is the key to trusting Him in uncertain times.

*Learning God's ways as He reveals His attributes through the pages of Scripture is the key to trusting Him in uncertain times.*

The prophet Isaiah reveals this about God's character: "Therefore the LORD waits to be gracious to you, and therefore he exalts himself to show mercy to you. For the LORD is a God of justice; blessed are all those who wait for him" (Isaiah 30:18 ESV).

God's ways are so different from ours. He will bring about what we might think is a trial to redirect our path toward His plan for our lives—and ultimately His blessing if we walk in obedience to that plan. Do you know God's character so well that you will trust Him if you find yourself without work? Or with having to reestablish your family in an unfamiliar place? How will knowing God through Bible study and prayer prepare you to trust Him in uncertain times?

# 17

# From Hopeless to Hopeful

### Nick and Kanae

*'ll never find anyone to marry me.*

Nick was convinced he'd be single forever. With no known medical reason for the condition, he was born without arms or legs. Throughout his childhood, Nick not only dealt with the typical challenges of school and adolescence, but he also struggled with depression and loneliness. He constantly wondered why he was different from all the other kids. He questioned the purpose of life, or if he even had a purpose.

With all the challenges of living without limbs, Nick fell to the lowest point of his life. At only ten years old he attempted suicide, but God had other plans for him. As He began to work on Nick's young heart, Nick resolved to never give up again.

According to Nick, the victory over his struggles—as well as his strength and passion for life today—can be credited to his faith in God. His family, friends, and the many people he has encountered along the journey have inspired him to carry on as well.

God began to give Nick opportunities to share his faith in a big way, and traveling the world and sharing the gospel became his passion. Crowds of people flocked to hear Nick's inspiring story of overcoming life without limbs, and countless people have surrendered their hearts to Christ as a result of Nick's evangelistic ministry.

As his public ministry grew, Nick hoped for a wife to minister alongside him. But with no arms to hold a woman, he thought marriage was out of his grasp. Nick recalled, "I felt like a burden to my parents during my childhood, and I never thought I would be able to be married to a person without feeling that way...I definitely had doubts that I'd ever get married—or that I'd ever meet anybody who would love to spend the rest of their life with me."

## THE SPARK

One night while Nick was speaking at a small event in Dallas, his eyes fell on a beautiful woman seated in the audience. As he continued sharing his motivational message, he had to force himself to look away from the attractive dark eyes locked onto his.

Kanae, the lovely woman in the audience, also sensed an immediate connection. "There was definitely a spark and a strong attraction from the first moment I locked eyes with Nick."

After the event Kanae and Nick chatted. Nick felt an immediate attraction to Kanae and Kanae was intrigued. She reminisced, "I was just amazed at this man of God who wanted to touch hearts, save souls, and make a difference in the world."

Later that night Nick texted his impression of Kanae to a mutual friend: "She is the most beautiful woman of God I've ever met in my life. She literally took my breath away!"

Nick failed to mention Kanae's name in the text, though, and his friend thought Nick was talking about Kanae's sister, Yoshie. When Nick's friend attempted to play matchmaker with Nick and Yoshie, things got a little confusing. Kanae recalled that the situation became so complicated she felt as though she were "trapped in a romantic comedy."

To complicate matters further, when she first met Nick, Kanae was involved in a relationship with another man. Although Kanae had a physical attraction to her current boyfriend, her heart was longing for something deeper.

When Kanae met Nick, she remembers, she was impressed with his humor and generosity, and she thought he was handsome. *He is not only boyfriend material, but he could be my husband.*

Soon Kanae began to sense inner turmoil over her relationship with her boyfriend, so she relied on God for answers. Kanae fasted and prayed to know what God would have her do. Finally, God's peace convinced her that the man she had been dating was not the one He would have her marry, so she broke off the relationship.

> *God's peace convinced her that the man she had been dating was not the one He would have her marry, so she broke off the relationship.*

Once Kanae was free she and Nick began to establish their friendship—which, Nick advised, "is critical to building a loving relationship."

## ELECTRIC

Eager to explore the possibility of a lifelong relationship, Nick and Kanae talked on the phone often and spent time together whenever possible. Nick said, "It was electric. When she stood by me, I just felt right."

Nick and Kanae both became confident in their love for each other. And Nick was in awe of the way Kanae showed her love toward him. In an interview with *The Christian Post*[1] Nick said, "She totally blew my mind with her love, thoughtfulness, and creativity during our courtship. She wrapped up a gift for me for my birthday in a way I had never even thought of. She slit open the corners of a cardboard box and kept the box in form by placing a ribbon around it where I could open it up by pulling on the ribbon with my mouth. It had no top but it was full of colored tissue paper so I couldn't see what was inside. It worked beautifully and perfectly. I did love the gift, but even before I tried opening up my very first present all by myself, I was honestly moved to tears with her amazing idea and touch of love like I had never felt before."

After a year of dating, Nick popped the question in a romantic setting that included a sailboat and cream puffs. He wanted to be the one to put the ring on Kanae's finger when he asked her to marry him, so he asked her if he could kiss her hand. Then he slipped the ring on her finger using his mouth. (Nick later disclosed that he almost gagged on the ring while it was in his mouth.)

Nick said, "Baby, I love you. Would you marry me and spend the rest of your life with me?" Kanae cried as she agreed to become Nick's wife.

Nick and Kanae announced their engagement to Nick's Facebook followers by posting a picture of themselves showing off Kanae's engagement ring. Nick's caption read, "The greatest blessing I've ever received after life, salvation, and a relationship with God: Introducing Nick and Kanae engaged!!! Thank you for your love, support and prayers."

Nick and Kanae wed and settled in their home in Southern California, where Kanae worked as a wife and keeper of their home. As with most newlyweds, they had challenges as they adjusted to married life. And Nick's unique condition presented unexpected needs. But Nick said his wife was prepared to handle them, and he was truly amazed by her love.

Before their wedding Nick and Kanae spent time in premarital counseling. Although no amount of counseling can completely prepare a couple for marriage, they also built their marriage foundation on Christ and daily deciding to give of themselves to meet the needs of the other.

Nick said, "I still wish I could do more things for her to also show how I love her. I do what I can. However, the greatest way to show my love is simply quality time together, honoring her family, and trying to do my best to be better than yesterday."

Nick continued to work on the messages for his ministry, Life Without Limbs, and on writing books. Recently, Nick and Kanae published a book they wrote together titled *Love Without Limits*.

On the day after their first wedding anniversary, God blessed Nick and Kanae with a son.

Nick said, "Kanae and I never thought that we as human beings had the capacity to love someone so much as we love our baby boy. It is a deeper and new dimension altogether that we love." Two years later Kanae gave birth to another beautiful baby boy.

As God grows Nick and Kanae's family, He is also growing their ministry to reach millions with the hope of the gospel of Jesus Christ. Nick and Kanae continue to focus on loving each other and their family. Nick candidly stated, "I am reminded daily of what I need to work on in my character as a man to be all that I want to be for her and our [family]."

*God knows, He hears your cries,*
*He feels your pain—and He has a plan.*

Nick shared the focus of their ministry together as a couple: "I think the biggest fear of all in one's life is to be alone. We want all to know that God is with us, and He does have a plan. It sometimes takes longer and takes turns down unexpected paths that lead to a future we could not foresee."

## PONDER THIS

Nick and Kanae's love story is a wonderful reminder of how God beautifully uses anyone willing to surrender to His perfect will. On Nick Vujicic's website, LifeWithoutLimbs.org, he makes this powerful statement: "God can use a life without limbs to show the world how to live a life without limits!"

In Psalm 139:13-14, the Bible says, "You created my inmost being; you knit me together in my mother's womb. I praise you because I am fearfully and wonderfully made; your works are wonderful, I know that full well" (NIV).

Take a moment to ponder how God is lovingly involved in creating each life for His purpose and His glory.

## ASK YOURSELF

What conditions in your life may be holding you back?

Do you have a child with a medical condition that leaves him or her discouraged? Where can you turn for encouragement? From Nick and Kanae's story, what hope can you offer your child?

Or like Nick, do you have a physical condition that causes you distress? Have you pulled away from the Lord because of it?

Resenting God, or focusing on the condition, is not how God wants you to live. He knows, He hears your cries, He feels your pain—and He has a plan.

Psalm 56:8 says, "You have kept count of my tossings; put my tears in your bottle. Are they not in your book?" (ESV). How does knowing the Lord is compassionate toward you when your tears fall help you trust Him with your circumstance?

*To learn more about Nick and Kanae's incredible story, visit www.life withoutlimbs.org or read their book,* Love Without Limits.[2]

# 18

# Happily Ever After... Again

## Walter and Sandy

W hile appearing on the program *LoveSavers*, I had the privilege of hearing hosts Walter and Sandy Fox recount their unique love story. Sandy laughed as she shared with me how she was on a date with another man the night she met Walter.

Sandy first laid eyes on Walter nearly 50 years ago. He was decked out in his naval officer uniform. At first sight, she was immediately smitten with his good looks. "When Walter walked in the door, I took one look at him in his uniform and it was just like in the comic books! I thought, *Wow–Bang–Pow!* Walter must have seen that in my eyes, because he walked right up to me and asked, 'Who are you here with?' I said, 'That fellow over there.' Walter said, 'Get rid of him.'"

Without a second thought Sandy went to her date and said, "Would you please leave now?"

"What do you mean? You're with me."

"Not anymore I'm not."

As Sandy delightfully told this story, she concluded by saying, "And that was our beginning. Walter took me by the hand and away we went."

Walter and Sandy were married in New York. I wish I could say theirs was a happily-ever-after fairy tale. But sadly, for the first nine years of their marriage they were more devoted to building their careers than to each other. Both were working in New York City in the fast-paced life of advertising and publishing. Sandy worked for a magazine and Walter had his own ad agency. Both were successful, at least in their careers.

> *For the first nine years of their marriage*
> *Walter and Sandy were more devoted to*
> *building their careers than to each other.*

Walter said, "For a number of reasons, after nine years of trying to make the marriage work, we divorced."

## THE DIVORCE

Sandy moved to New England with the children while Walter stayed in New York to run his advertising agency.

Walter said that, at that time, he knew something was missing in his heart and his soul. He sought out counsel, even from a psychiatrist in New York City. "I sat on the couch in the psychiatrist's office. Next to me was a battered tennis racket. The psychiatrist explained I was to use the tennis racket to beat the couch to get out my anger and frustrations."

While Walter did not find beating the couch with the racket useful, he did take to heart one piece of advice from the psychiatrist, who told him to read Psalm 23.

During this season of searching, Walter had looked to many things to fill the ache in his heart. He explored Eastern philosophy, looking for a guru. He attended EST training. He laughed as he told me this training required attendees to not go to the restroom for the entire two days of the training. He left EST with the understanding, "We are all victims."

Walter continued to look for answers in Transcendental Meditation, Mind Freedom, and several other false religions. "I was just looking for love in all the wrong places. As I was pursuing looking for this truth, I found myself reading the Bible, of all things—because many of the occult books I had been reading talked of Jesus as a high master and a prophet. I was raised Roman Catholic, although I did not know Jesus in a personal way."

## THE ANSWER

About his journey to know Jesus, Walter said, "I wanted to know more about this man Jesus. The Bible says the Word of God is the substance of things hoped for. It is living, and the more I read it, the more it began to stir my heart to want to know Truth. These words in the Bible were alive, doing something inside of me. They were building my faith. Unbeknownst to me, God was doing a work in my heart to change me and draw me to believe in Jesus. I was a seeker looking for a precious pearl. As I searched, God was speaking to me and dispelling everything the occult had been trying to teach me."

One day, in one of the occult books Walter had been reading, he came across this statement: "When you see the face of God you will know truth."

Walter said to himself, *That's it. When I see God's face, I will know Him and I will know the truth.* But he had no idea how to discover the face of God.

As Walter was crossing the street near Grand Central Station one morning, he had an urge to go into a little church he passed. He decided to go inside just to be quiet, sit, meditate, and think about his life—and about his children and his family.

As Walter sat, he picked up a booklet he found nearby. At the bottom of every page was one line of scripture. On one page Walter read, "Him that cometh to me I will in no wise cast out" (John 6:37 KJV).

Walter said, "After I read that scripture, I began to cry. Totally moved emotionally. This emotion came about after I read the Word of God. Because it is alive and active and divides soul from spirit. At that moment I was changed forever."

He continued, "As I walked out of that church into the bustle of New York City, I was oblivious to the incredible energy and activity all around me. I was so smitten with God's peace, so changed, so powerfully moved by this encounter with God. In a moment of time, my surrender to Christ changed me that day—not only in that moment, but for all eternity. I even forgot to go to the bank!"

Walter remembers sitting at his desk back in his office with an incredible peace. His passion for building his company and climbing to the top no longer mattered to him.

As he sat a friend and coworker happened by his office. After observing Walter's unusual sense of peace, he asked, "What happened to you?"

Walter quietly answered, "I think I just met Jesus."

Walter's friend replied, "Oh no..." and quickly scurried away.

After that experience Walter began to attend Bible studies, praying and reading the Word, all the while asking questions and growing in his faith. "I had a real born-again experience. I was a new species in Christ—a new person, forever changed!"

With Walter's transformed life came questions about his marriage. He asked church leaders what he should do about his broken marriage, and he read Christian books about the subject, but he was still unclear as to what God would have him do. Then one day as Walter was sitting quietly waiting on the Lord, his Bible in his lap opened to the book of Hosea, the words seemed to leap off the page: "Rejoice in the wife of your youth." In that moment Walter knew God was telling him, "Return to the wife of your youth."

Walter knew this was God's answer for his situation. But he wondered how God could heal their marriage. By this time Walter and Sandy had been divorced for seven years. They lived in different parts of the country and they were pursuing very different interests.

Walter said, "To drop off the kids for visitation, we would meet in New Haven. She was in Providence; I was in New York."

As he told this story, Walter turned to Sandy and laughingly said, "You were nice sometimes and sometimes you were not."

Laughing as well, Sandy agreed with Walter's recollection of the situation.

## THE TURNING POINT

As Sandy recalled observing this season of change in Walter's life, she said to him, "I remember at that time I was feeling compassion toward you. I seemed to be seeing something change in you that I didn't understand. So I invited you to come and spend Christmas with me and the children. And you came and you gave us all presents. But then it was a time of confusion. I felt like I had other things going on and I felt I needed to leave our family time to go to Connecticut."

She turned to me. "Walter got terribly angry and stomped off. Then a little while later a telephone call came…"

Walter clarified. "We are a work in progress. God is always working on our hearts, thoughts, behavior. I was a new Christian at the time. So my expectation was that God spoke to me to return to the wife of my youth. And I expected Sandy to return to me with open arms to restore our marriage. And here Sandy had a friend she had to go and meet. I got into my Chevy and I drove down to I-95, headed back to New York. I was angry, upset, disappointed, and my expectations were off the wall.

"Along the way, God spoke to me and said 'Walter, stop the car and call Sandy and apologize to her.' I started to weep. I couldn't even drive because I couldn't see where I was going. In those days there were no cell phones. I had to pull over and search for enough change to call Sandy on a pay phone. Fortunately, she still happened to be at home.

"Smitten by the power of God's love that overshadowed me, I said, 'Sandy, I want to apologize for the way I reacted to you. What I said to you was something I shouldn't have said.'"

Sandy couldn't believe what she was hearing. For as long as she had known Walter, he had been an angry man. She could hardly believe the gentle tenderness she heard in his voice. "I sensed there was something different in this apology. It may have been the Holy Spirit helping me see it. The change in Walter is what encouraged me to actually look into whatever it was that Walter had been seeking."

After that Sandy started going to church, taking the children with her. Eventually Sandy surrendered her heart to Christ. This was the beginning of the healing of their broken marriage.

## HAPPILY EVER AFTER…AGAIN

Soon Walter and Sandy married for the second time. As they renewed their journey—this time with God as the center of their relationship—they gave up all the career pursuits that had so damaged their marriage the first time around.

Once an important executive who traveled to many places others would envy, Walter now found himself and his family living in a small Brooklyn apartment. Walter remembers hearing the mice and cockroaches scurry across the ceiling. Sandy added that they eventually got cats and that took care of the mice, but not the roaches.

But even without all the finer things in life, Walter and Sandy were unbelievably happy. As God would have it, their apartment was right next to a ministry that became, as Walter put it, "just what we needed. Living next door to this ministry was intensive care—like a spiritual hospital for us."

It was at this fellowship that Walter and Sandy learned to pray diligently. And they went to a different meeting almost every night of the week. From Bible studies, along with counseling from the ministry next door, they were enjoying the love and care of the body of Christ.

Walter explained. "We learned that God always gives you exactly what you need when you are willing to obey His will. He will provide everything you need to facilitate your growth. All these details and experiences had to do with God's eternal purpose to change us from who we were to who He wanted us to become."

Over the years God has blessed Walter and Sandy with a ministry to help struggling married couples reconcile. They host their own radio program called *LoveSaversRADIO*, and Walter wrote a book about their story, *Return to the Wife of Your Youth*, to help others find hope for a broken marriage.

*"What we cannot do alone, we can do
if we are attached to the Lord."*

The theme scripture for Walter and Sandy's LoveSavers ministry is Ecclesiastes 4:12 (esv): "A cord of three strands is not quickly broken." Sandy said, "What we cannot do alone, we can do if we are attached to the Lord." This couple's reconciled marriage is certainly a picture of this truth.

## PONDER THIS

Is your marriage so far gone you don't think anything can save it? If God can transform Walter and Sandy's marriage, He is powerful enough to help your marriage. Notice Walter was the one who first came to Christ. When Sandy didn't respond to him the way he expected, his initial reaction was anger. But Walter humbled himself and asked Sandy's forgiveness, and his Christlike attitude opened Sandy's heart to want to know more about following Jesus.

## ASK YOURSELF

What hope can you find in hearing Walter and Sandy's story of reconciliation? If, like Walter was, you've been searching for love and answers in all the wrong places, won't you take some time to consider seeking to know Jesus for yourself? The Bible says, "Now is the day of salvation" (2 Corinthians 6:2 ESV), and maybe now is your time to surrender to Christ.

# 19

# Something Set Apart

## Steve and Becky

I t seemed as though it was only a matter of time before Becky and her boyfriend would become engaged. Everyone assumed they were a natural fit. Steve felt the same way about the young woman he had been dating for nearly two years. For Becky and Steve marriage seemed imminent—but not to each other.

How wrong they both were! Instead of leading to the altar, both relationships came to an unexpected end.

The disappointment that followed—for both Steve and Becky—was heartbreaking. So much so that neither of them sought to date anyone for a while. Becky had her job at Universal Studios in their state of California and was actively involved in the disability ministry at the church she and Steve both attended. Steve had a full load of university courses and was teaching both a Sunday school class and a midweek Bible study for the deaf. And both took part in a lot of ministry activities at their church, including those hosted by Joni and Friends, the ministry of Joni Eareckson Tada.

Steve and Becky's paths crossed frequently because they both attended the same college Bible study on Friday nights. And on Sunday mornings, Becky served as a sign-language interpreter, while Steve, who is hearing impaired, sat in the section reserved for the deaf members of their church. This crisscrossing of paths went on for quite some time. Becky recalled, "We became such good friends, we can't really pinpoint when our first date was."

But they do remember the night that, for her birthday, Steve took Becky out to a live performance of *Peter Pan* at the Pantages Theater in Hollywood. When Becky met Steve at the door wearing a beautiful dress, her own beauty took his breath away. And Steve was ever-so-handsome all decked out in a tuxedo. Although they had made dinner reservations at a fine restaurant nearby, unexpected delays forced a change of plans, and they had time for only a quick burger stop before heading to the show. Heads turned as they entered Carl's Jr. dressed to the hilt, which prompted a lot of amused looks and friendly laughs.

Along the way in their friendship, their hearts became more closely knit. But they weren't even holding hands yet, or exchanging notes or doing anything else that usually accompanies a relationship growing more serious. Not because they weren't ready for it. Becky was dropping quite a few hints, but Steve was the overly cautious type. He wanted to make sure he wasn't reading too much into those hints.

Yes, Steve was ever so cautious—for a few reasons. For the most part he had always been a shy and reserved person. And after the painful break up of his previous dating relationship, he didn't want to experience the hurt that could come if a relationship didn't work out. And finally, he was having a hard time believing this incredibly gracious and attractive woman really was showing more than a friendship kind of interest in him.

It took a while for their very good friendship to move up another notch.

Until that night at their church college group's winter weekend retreat.

Have you ever had two friends you knew liked each other but at least one of them seemed unaware of how the other one felt? One of Becky's friends was in just that situation. She knew Becky had feelings for Steve and was dropping hints to him, but Steve seemed oblivious to those hints. One night at the retreat, Becky's friend pulled Steve aside and spelled things out a bit more clearly. She assured him, "No, the hints Becky has been dropping aren't merely coincidental. And yes, there really is something more than just a friendship here."

Once Steve had the assurance that Becky returned his affections, he was happy to pursue a relationship with her, and their relationship grew quickly. Because both were so busy—Steve with school and Becky with work—and because both were so heavily involved in ministry activities, their dating life revolved almost entirely around their church life. That meant an enormous part of their relationship growth took place in the context of spiritual growth.

There's a saying that when two people in a relationship are both actively pursuing God, as they grow closer to the Lord they will also grow closer to each other. Imagine a triangle with the man at the lower left angle, the woman at the lower right angle, and God at the top. As the man and woman each look upward to God and make Him their first priority in all things, they will not only move closer to Him, but also to each other.

> *When two people in a relationship are both actively pursuing God, as they grow closer to the Lord they will also grow closer to each other.*

That's what happened with Steve and Becky.

## PINING AWAY AND LOSING SLEEP

The couple spent many memorable times together: Date nights to see *Chariots of Fire* and *Lady and the Tramp*. Wednesday evening services at their church. College volleyball at the church gym. Helping out at disability ministry events at amusement parks and other places. Three months after that winter retreat, Steve was convinced Becky was the woman he wanted to marry. He was finding it more and more difficult to focus on his studies and sleep at night. He sensed within himself a restlessness that wouldn't go away until he asked for her hand in marriage.

Steve began to ponder how he should go about proposing to Becky, and where. At a nice restaurant? A park? The beach? As he considered the possibilities, he thought of one spot that would symbolize what was so important to both of them—the one place that, more than any other, had a key part in shaping who they were and why they were drawn to each other.

The church Steve and Becky attended was well known for its exceptional Bible teaching—teaching that had powerfully influenced their lives (and would continue to do so even after they moved nearly one thousand miles away from Los Angeles).

Steve decided to propose to Becky at the foot of the pulpit in their church's worship center. At this pulpit God's Word was clearly proclaimed, leading unsaved people to Christ and believers to spiritual maturity. They both wanted a God-centered relationship, and they knew the key to a growing and fulfilling marriage was to keep God at the forefront of all they did.

One evening, after a family gathering, Steve suggested to Becky they swing by the church before he dropped her off at her house. They went into the worship center, and he walked Becky to the foot of the pulpit. As he nervously cleared his throat and got ready to propose, a good friend of theirs on the janitorial staff at the church entered the building. This friend was excited to see them, and their visit went five… ten…fifteen…twenty minutes long. This wasn't going the way Steve planned!

Finally, the friend left, and Steve could propose. And yes, Becky accepted!

## WORTH THE WAIT

Their hope was to marry at the beginning of Steve's senior year in college. But their parents felt strongly that Steve should graduate first. This meant that instead of a six-month engagement, theirs would last more than 14 months. Steve said, "We knew that honoring our parents was important, and we wanted their full support. So we set the wedding date for one week after graduation. Of course, being engaged at the one-year point *before* your wedding day means you can celebrate your 'first' anniversary a full year before the wedding!"

When the big day finally arrived, Steve and Becky once again stood at the foot of the pulpit—this time ready to become one in marriage. Because Becky was partly of Jewish heritage, they had asked their pastor to refer to, in the wedding ceremony, the Hebrew term *kiddushin*, which is the first stage of the Jewish wedding or betrothal process. It basically means "consecration" or "sanctification."

*To consecrate* means "to set something apart." And in a Christian marriage, the man and woman are fully consecrated to each other. To speak of *kiddushin*, then, is similar to saying, "I am totally set apart for you and devoted to you." It speaks of a union where two people are completely surrendered to each other.

That's how Steve and Becky wanted to view their marriage—a forever promise to be devoted to each other, which is God's design for marriage.

## FINDING A HOME

After Steve and Becky had their first child, they wanted to move into a home of their own. But living in Los Angeles was expensive. They spent many months looking for a house, but they simply couldn't afford one.

When they were about to give up, Steve's mom called to let them know about a foreclosed home listed in the classifieds for a price far below even the least expensive homes in the area. Steve and Becky immediately called the bank that had title over the home. They were told to show up at the house and make a bid to a bank official, who would meet them there.

Upon arriving at the house, it quickly became apparent why the price was so low. The house was horribly dilapidated and needed serious repairs.

As it turned out, someone else showed up, too—a professional builder who wanted to fix up the house and quickly turn it for a profit. His bid was submitted first, which meant Steve and Becky were second in line. The bank said that after a three-day waiting period, the winning bidder would get the home.

To Steve, those three days were like three years. He was nervous and couldn't sleep. He told Becky, "I just *know* the bank is going to give the house to the builder. His bid was first, and he has more money."

But Becky was perfectly calm. "If God wants us to have the house, He will work it out so we get it." To her, it was as simple as that. God would either open the door or close it. She was at total peace, while Steve was biting his nails.

Surprisingly, for reasons Steve and Becky still don't know, the builder's bid fell through. The bank called on day three. "Would you like to buy the house?"

Would they ever!

Steve said, "Looking back on that experience has been a lifelong lesson in learning to trust God no matter what."

When the odds seemed impossibly against them, God came through and provided a home. It needed three years of fixing up, and it was a tiny and humble abode, but Steve and Becky treasured this place they could call their own. And in the nearly 35 years since, Steve has repeatedly remembered the simple faith Becky had in God's provision—a faith that continues to remind him to rest in the Lord no matter how uncertain life gets.

## OVER THE YEARS

God blessed Steve and Becky with three sons. Looking back, both agree the highlight of parenting for them was being actively involved in their sons' school and sports activities. They made sure to be available for all the behind-the-scenes preparations as well as to support them in their endeavors. They recalled, "We believe the two keys to a happy family are staying engaged with the kids and getting involved with their interests. Yes, doing this required a lot of time and energy. But it truly was an impressionable way to say, 'We love you' to our children."

Becky and Steve are the first to admit they weren't perfect parents, but their love and level of involvement with their children has reaped lifelong blessings in the strong relationship they now have with their adult sons. Steve shared, "We learned how our devotion to support our kids gave them the security and confidence that no matter what—even when things don't go well—Mom and Dad will be there."

While raising their boys, Steve was blessed with a job as an editor for a Christian publishing company. And Becky was also given a position as the company's receptionist. Over the years this has allowed her to work alongside Steve, available to assist him whenever his hearing impairment required her help.

The two are a powerful example of how loving Christ as a priority of life shines forth in total devotion to one another in marriage. And that love has spilled over onto their sons, daughters-in-law, and now in devotion to their grandchildren.

Some years ago a painter created an artistic rendering of the pulpit where Steve proposed to Becky. The painting was a tribute to the longtime faithful teaching of God's Word from that pulpit, and it now hangs in the office center of their former church. Steve and Becky have a professionally reproduced print of that same painting in their home. The image serves as a gentle reminder of where it all began—where they met, how God brought their lives together, and where they covenanted to make their lives one. And it reminds them as well that God and His Word are the wellspring of every blessing believers have the privilege of enjoying in both life and marriage.

## PONDER THIS

After both Steve and Becky felt the disappointment of a broken relationship, God showed them His plan when He knit their hearts together as they served in ministry. As the two continued to make loving Christ the priority of their lives, God grew their adoration for each other in a way that brought honor to Him.

*God grew their adoration for each other in a way that brought honor to Him.*

Ponder how carefully God is involved in the details of our lives and how His providence caused Steve and Becky's paths to cross, not only to honor Him through their devotion to each other, but also to encourage their children as they enjoyed the security of their parents' deep love for Christ and for each other.

When Steve and Becky waited to see if the Lord would bless them with a house, Becky's confidence in God's provision bolstered her husband's faith. When life seems to not make sense, when finances aren't measuring up, or circumstances are uncertain, is your faith so grounded in Christ that your confidence in Him uplifts your husband?

Proverbs 3:5-6 says, "Trust in the LORD with all your heart, and lean not on your own understanding; in all your ways acknowledge Him, and He shall direct your paths." Ask yourself if you are leaning on your own understanding or are committed to look to God, rather than circumstances, to rest in His plans and provision.

20

## Until the Final Breath

### Curt and Vi

O ne of my favorite love stories of all time is my friend Vi's. I met Vi at a pastors' wives conference 17 years ago, right after my husband accepted the position of senior pastor at First Baptist Church in Patterson, California.

When I met Vi I knew I had found a treasure. Her love for Christ and for her husband was priceless. Her adoration for the ministry of pastor's wife made me want to become just like her.

### THE DIVINE WALTZ

Vi was married for 42 years to Curt—the love of her life. When I asked Vi to tell me about how she and Curt met, she said, "We were in college, on a choir tour. I played the piano and he was going into music ministry, so we were a good fit." She jokingly added, "Although, when you play the piano and you marry a minister, you're never quite sure if he married you for love or because he needed a pianist!"

Throughout their married life Vi and Curt served the Lord in full-time ministry. Vi often referred to their marriage as a waltz through life, divinely choreographed by the Lord. Their waltz came to an end when Curt was diagnosed with cancer at age 68. As his health failed, Vi never left his side.

On the last day of his life, Curt looked to his sweetheart and said, "Vi, am I dying?" To which Vi tearfully responded, "Yes, dear, you are dying."

And then in the joyful spirit Curt so adored, Vi whispered, "Curt, you are going home to see Jesus! What is the first thing you want to say to Him when you see His face?"

Curt closed his eyes and smiled as he considered the moment he would stand in the presence of the Lord. And then without hesitation, he looked into Vi's gentle eyes and said, "I am going to thank Him for giving me *you*."

> "I am going to thank Him for giving me you."

That night Curt went home to be with the Lord. To be read at Curt's celebration of life, Vi penned this poem.

### The Waltz

"Will you come and dance with me?" he asked me oh so tenderly,
"And waltz with me around the floor like
no two ever danced before?"
I smiled at him; my heart skipped a beat and
before I realized it, I was on my feet.
Accepting his invitation seemed so right—
I was willing to dance all night.

He looked to the Maestro and said, "Conductor, if you please"
And at his direction, the orchestra played with the greatest of ease
The most beautiful waltz I'd ever heard
And we danced and danced without saying a word.

We both knew when the music began that we
were a part of a much larger plan,
And this waltz that we started just minutes
ago was the first of a lifetime of dances
To show that we were becoming partners for life;
Not just on the dance floor, but as husband and wife.

I followed his lead as the music played on and we
moved 'cross the floor in complete unison.
What freedom I felt with his hand in mine, keeping in step, stepping in time.
The future was bright for two people that night
who waltzed as though dancing on air.
Life was just grand while holding his hand
and gone were all worries and cares.

As the music played on and the clock ticked away,
nighttime approached at the close of the day
And the music took on a different mood; and
we found ourselves with a new attitude.
We were tired, without a doubt, and found
that even good things wear you out!
But when one would faint, the other was strong
and together we faced each new song.

There were times, I'll admit, when I wanted to
quit, But how could I leave him alone?
We'd partnered for life and I was his wife, "flesh
of his flesh and bone of his bone."
He was my "head" and I, his "helpmate," We've
waltzed now for so many years.
I've laughed when he laughed and cried when
he cried, shedding innumerable tears.

Now we've become one and though the dancing is done, we still make quite a smart pair.
I'll never regret that day when we met and he
asked me to spin 'round the floor.
Sometimes it seemed slow, the music you
know, and other times it was so very fast.
But together we stayed whatever was played and
looking back, I thank God for the past.

One, two, three—one, two, three—It's
the rhythm of the waltz you see;

One Conductor, plus two partners, make a unit of three.
The Conductor selected the tunes and tempo for each melody.
And side by side, we simply complied with
the music He played faithfully.

## PONDER THIS

Consider Curt's final words to his beloved Vi: "I'm going to thank Him for giving me *you*." Does your heart long to hear your husband feels this same way about you? I regularly speak at women's events and marriage conferences.[1] Whenever I tell Vi and Curt's love story, I can't help but cry over the sweetness of their love. And across audiences, women's tears fall. Why? I think because each of us wants to build a love like that. We know the wife we long to be—the wife we have meant to be—but somewhere along the way we've lost our way.

Titus 2:4 calls older women to teach the younger women how to love their husbands. I have made a lifelong practice of befriending older women who have spent their lives loving well Christ, their husbands, and their children. I'm confident the friendships I've made with these older women have had a profound influence on guiding me toward becoming the wife, mother, and woman I long to be.

## ASK YOURSELF

What about you? Does Vi's love story tug at your heartstrings to be the kind of wife your husband will thank God for at the end of his life—let alone each and every day of his life? Rather than simply longing to be a better wife, you must actively take steps toward becoming the wife you hope to be. Take to heart God's Titus 2 plan to help you by looking to older women for help—women whose marriages you want to emulate.

*Rather than simply longing to be a better wife, you must actively take steps toward becoming the wife you hope to be.*

Maybe you relate well to Vi's story because you have built a marriage that reflects Christ's selfless love. While I'm happy for your accomplishment, remember that you are not free to simply rest on your happy life. God is calling you to minister to a younger generation of women desperate to learn the secret to building a happy marriage that honors Christ. In my speaking, I regularly meet young women who say they can't find any godly Christian women to mentor them. However old you are, there is always a younger woman who needs to learn from your experience, both from your successes and your failures. (I don't know about you, but I teach more passionately from my failures than I do from my successes.)

Won't you prayerfully consider how God would have you mentor a younger woman? Giving her a copy of this book may be a great place to start.

# My Favorite Love Stories

## I Saved the Best For Last!

Watching two people fall in love is delightful, wouldn't you agree? As a mother, I have had the wonderful privilege of observing how God brought spouses to each of our four children. There was something incredible about watching the Lord work to answer the prayers my husband, Steve, and I prayed for them. From the day they were born, we regularly asked God to lead each of them to a spouse who loved Christ and would live to serve Him all their days.

The next four love stories will be from my perspective as a mom watching my kids fall in love. I hope you enjoy these stories as much as I love telling them. Oh, and…you may want to grab a tissue.

# 21

# Breaking the Bro Code

## Estevan and Kayla

ShannenNatashaPhotography

Our youngest daughter, Kayla, was 14 years old when her heart first pitter-pattered for Estevan. They were at a church coffeehouse the night she noticed him. He was about her brother Brandon's age—two years older than Kayla—so she was pretty sure he hadn't even taken notice of the little blond girl playing board games with her girlfriends that night.

Estevan—Stev to his friends— had agreed to come to the coffeehouse at his friend's church. Estevan had been raised to believe in God, but he had no understanding of God's desire to have a relationship with him. Although he had once gone forward at a church to pray, the idea of God wanting to know him personally seemed far-fetched to him.

However, Estevan enjoyed his friends who were Christians, so he had no hesitation about attending a free coffeehouse that promised live music, fun, and fellowship. Living in a small town his whole life, Estevan was always up for something new to do with friends. He couldn't have known this night would be a catalyst that would change his life—forever.

Brandon and Estevan became fast friends. The two had much in common with their kind, gentle manner and love for music. The more time Brandon and Estevan spent together, the more Estevan was exposed to what it really meant to live in relationship with Christ. It wasn't long before Estevan fully surrendered his life to Jesus.

Church became a place Estevan loved to attend, and he couldn't get enough of learning from the Bible and applying Truth to his life. As a musician, he had found true satisfaction in using his talent to play worship music rather than secular music.

As their friendship grew, Brandon often invited Estevan, along with several other boys, up to our ranch for a weekend. The boys would shoot guns, play paintball, and ride dirt bikes, thoroughly enjoying their time together in the mountains. Kayla, too, had girlfriends come up for weekends, and in the evenings all the kids would play games, watch movies, and just hang out.

My husband, Steve, and I realized how having a bunch of teens spending the night presented challenges to keep couples from pairing off, but we also preferred our kids to fellowship with their friends at our home rather than any place we couldn't supervise their activities. During that season, lots of prayer for wisdom and late nights of staying up with the kids became a habit—not to mention having many talks with the kids about how God blesses the marriages of His followers who remain sexually pure.

After a time, it was apparent that Estevan was becoming interested in Kayla, but he tried to ignore it. Liking Kayla would present problems. First, Estevan thought to himself, *There's the bro-code. You don't date your best friend's sister.*

Kayla's cousin, Adrian, was also close friends with Estevan and Brandon, which only compounded the whole "bro-code" concern. Then there was their age difference. Estevan was only a year and a half older than Kayla, but he was two years ahead of her in school, which made their age difference seem too extreme.

And also there was the fact that Kayla's father was Estevan's pastor. Dating the pastor's daughter would certainly be intimidating. So with all those concerns, Estevan kept his feelings to himself and continued to hang out with the group—for a time.

## TIME IS ON OUR SIDE

The more time Kayla and Estevan spent together, the more their admiration grew. Kayla observed Estevan's kind heart as he interacted with their friends, and Estevan enjoyed watching Kayla's bubbly personality. Both realized they were too young to think about "forever," but secretly each was considering the possibility.

One day Estevan reached over and held Kayla's hand. She could hardly believe it! She had wondered, *What would it be like if Estevan liked me too?* She now had a glimmer of hope that he just might be attracted to her as well.

When the two finally talked about their feelings for each other, Kayla couldn't have been happier. But she also was deeply concerned about how this revelation would be welcomed by her brother, and more importantly by her father. Steve had made it very clear to Kayla that she would not be allowed to "like" a boy, let alone date anyone, for many years. She knew they would need her dad's blessing if they were going to be boyfriend and girlfriend, but Kayla was pretty sure she knew what her father's response would be.

## THE TALK

Estevan was not one for keeping secrets. When he had something on his mind, his practice was to talk it through with whomever was involved. Estevan's feelings for Kayla would be no different.

One night after youth group, I was sitting in the front office outside of Steve's office while he was meeting with someone. Several times I noticed Estevan walk in to see if Steve was still unavailable. Each time he went back out to fellowship with his friends, only to come checking again and again.

Poor Estevan looked nervous, and I couldn't help but feel for him. It was apparent to me that he was working up the courage to have a talk with Kayla's dad about his feelings for our little girl. I have adored Estevan from the very first time I met him. His smile and love for life were absolutely precious. So to be honest, when Estevan and Kayla showed signs of liking each other, I secretly rooted for them, even though I knew they were too young to start a relationship. But I also asked God to reveal to them His timing and will for their relationship—if He even wanted them to have one.

Estevan poked his head in to check once more and found Steve's office door open. As he walked past me, he invited me to join him in Steve's office. "I have something I want to talk to you about."

As the door closed and we settled into our seats, Estevan's apprehension became apparent to Steve. Normally Steve would take the initiative in a situation where a counselee was nervous and needed prompting. Not so with poor Estevan.

In my observation, Steve had obviously "taken off his pastor hat" and put on his "dad hat" for this conversation. If Estevan was going to talk to him about his daughter, Steve was going to make him man-up and take the initiative. Everything in me wanted to jump in and disarm the tension, but I knew this was a man-to-man thing. Estevan had just invited me to come in for moral support.

Finally, Estevan looked at Steve and said, "I have feelings for your daughter."

Steve responded, "Which daughter?" Knowing full well Estevan was not talking about Kayla's 20-year-old sister, I was dying. Steve was not gonna make this easy on poor Estevan.

Estevan's eyes got real big as he clarified. "Oh. Kayla. I have feelings for Kayla."

And did Steve throw the boy a bone? No. "Feelings? What do you mean by feelings?"

"I like Kayla."

After a long pause, Steve said, "You like Kayla, huh? So what do you want to do about that? She's not old enough to get married, and she's not allowed to date, so what do you propose?"

Attempting to throw Estevan a lifeline, I jumped into the conversation. "You know, Estevan, you couldn't have chosen a more difficult relationship to pursue. Kayla is your best friend's sister, and your pastor's daughter."

Estevan replied, "I know. I have tried really hard not to like her, but I just can't help it. I like her a lot!"

What mom wouldn't love to hear a young man say that about her daughter? The adoration I had for Estevan only multiplied.

Steve, on the other hand, was less than enamored by the idea of his baby girl and this high school boy having "feelings" for each other, and he said as much.

After what seemed like an eternity, Steve explained how he couldn't stop them from liking one another, but Kayla was much too young to date and they would not be allowed to call each other "boyfriend and girlfriend." And Steve made clear there would be no alone time allowed for the two.

Estevan told Steve he understood the stipulations and would respect his wishes. He and Kayla would spend time together in a group setting and honor Steve's instruction to not tell others they were boyfriend and girlfriend.

With that, Estevan got up and hugged both of us ever so sweetly. Did I mention how much I loved that boy?

After Estevan left, Steve told me, "Kayla is too young to have feelings for him." When I reminded Steve I was Kayla's age when I met him, and I knew he was "the one," Steve asked me not to tell Kayla about that.

I laughed and explained how Kayla already knew our love story and was fully aware of how young I was when I fell for her daddy. Steve and I prayed for God to give us His wisdom to know how to direct these two young lovebirds. We knew they genuinely cared for each other and truly had a love for Christ.

## ONE DAY

As time went on and Brandon processed the betrayal he felt over his best buddy falling for his sister, Kayla and Estevan continued to honor Steve's wishes in their relationship.

One day Estevan mentioned to me that he wanted to learn to drive a car with a stick shift. I happened to have an old model BMW with four-on-the-floor, so I offered to teach him how to drive my car. It was a beautiful spring day, and since the car was a convertible, it seemed a perfect day to take a drive. I handed my keys to Estevan and said, "Let's go."

Kayla joined us in the backseat. As we drove and Estevan was getting the hang of shifting while using the clutch, we began a lighthearted visit. Then Estevan turned to me and said, "Why does Steve hate me?"

Poor boy. He was still trying to process why Steve wouldn't let Kayla be his girlfriend. On several occasions Estevan had invited Kayla to come to his house after school to hang out. Steve always said no.

I looked into Estevan's eyes and said, "Estevan, Steve loves you a lot. He loves Kayla too. He sees that the two of you deeply care for each other. The problem is you are both *so* young. Maybe God will allow you to marry each other one day, but that will be a long way off. Steve's desire is to help you and Kayla discern God's will in what He would have for your relationship. And Steve and I both know that if we allow you to spend time alone as a couple, the odds are you won't remain sexually pure over the many years you will have to wait to be married, if that's what God has for the two of you."

Kayla's eyes got as big as saucers as I went on. "It's not just about not having sex until you're married. It's about remaining pure so God can lead each of you by His Spirit. If you involve yourselves in sex now, not only will you be sinning against God and His perfect plan for your lives, but you will also be quenching the Spirit so you won't be able to discern if God would even want you to marry each other. Does that make sense?"

The look on Estevan's face told me he comprehended what I was saying. He took it to heart and then said, "I understand. I get it."

With that, Estevan seemed relieved to have a better understanding of the reasons for Steve's reservations about allowing them alone time.

## SCHOOL DAYS

During Estevan's senior year we allowed Kayla to attend public high school for tenth grade. We lived 45 minutes up a mountain from the school, so up to that point Kayla had been on independent study.

Before Kayla obtained Steve's permission to make this change, she had to agree to some requirements. One requirement was that she and Estevan would still not be allowed to tell their friends they were "boyfriend and girlfriend." And they still had to agree not to spend time alone as a couple.

At this point the two had earned our trust in so many ways, but we knew the temptations they would face, and we still hoped to help them honor Christ in their relationship.

Steve and I were also aware of the possibility of a "Romeo and Juliet complex" if we put our foot down and said, "We forbid you to have feelings for each other." In 18 years of youth ministry, we had learned a thing or two about guiding kids through dating, yet we regularly sought the Lord for His wisdom for Kayla and Estevan's relationship.

## TRAGEDY STRIKES

At school Kayla and Estevan spent every break together and enjoyed meeting for lunch. Estevan was happy to have the cute little blonde on campus and made it a point to walk her to each class.

Estevan was very attractive and well known on campus, so the girls couldn't help but notice how much attention he was paying the new girl. Many were surprised when Kayla explained how she and Estevan cared for each other but were choosing to remain sexually pure until marriage.

One day Estevan's mother died without warning. Kayla and Estevan were with some friends after school when he got the call. His father was working out of town, so Estevan called Steve to meet him at home, where his brother had found their mother.

Amid Estevan's heart-wrenching experience, Steve and I watched him press into his relationship with Christ, looking to Jesus in his grief. I remember telling Steve, "How often do you get to watch the young man who loves your daughter walk through the biggest trial of his life?"

## FIRST COMES LOVE

Estevan and Kayla's first official date was on Valentine's Day. Steve had granted Estevan permission to take Kayla out to dinner—just the two of them. Kayla was unbelievably excited! The two were so cute as they drove away for their date.

Estevan graduated high school and went to a local college while Kayla spent two more years in high school. Somewhere in that time Steve granted Kayla permission to refer to Estevan as her boyfriend.

As young couples often do, Estevan and Kayla broke up and got back together a couple of times. But by the time Kayla graduated high school the two were sure they were in love and would be together forever. Kayla determined to attend the local college where Estevan was a student.

Again, Steve stepped in and asked Kayla to prayerfully consider going away to a Christian college for at least one year. Not only did we want Kayla to have the biblical foundation a year of Bible college would bring, but we wanted her and Estevan to have a year apart to prayerfully consider God's will for their future together.

Tearfully, Kayla agreed with her daddy that going away would be a good decision. On the day she left for college, we drove by Estevan's house so they could say good-bye. My heart ached for them as they embraced and cried over the idea of being apart. As we drove away Estevan couldn't help but think the little blonde girl may have just driven out of his life forever.

But God had other plans. Over the next semester Kayla grew in her walk with Christ as she studied the Bible and read several books with a sound biblical worldview. When she and Estevan visited over Skype, she told him all she was learning.

One day Estevan went to visit Kayla at college. He told her, "You should be with one of these guys studying to be a pastor."

She told him, "Knowing everything about the Bible is important, but being teachable and learning to be a godly husband is what is important to me."

Estevan replied, "Then I know what I need to do."

From that day on, Estevan took seriously his responsibility to prepare himself to lead Kayla spiritually if she would one day be his bride. He began studying the Word and applying it to his life.

Steve and I watched as Estevan emerged a strong, godly man. Somewhere along the way remaining sexually pure was no longer something the two agreed to only because it honored her parents' wishes. Rather, they kept themselves sexually pure because it honored Christ. As the two matured, we could hardly wait until they wed.

## THEN COMES MARRIAGE

Kayla had just turned 20 when Estevan finally popped the question.

Estevan planned a lovely day in San Francisco. He borrowed his father's Mercedes and drove Kayla to a spot in view of Golden Gate Bridge. Kayla was oblivious to Estevan's intentions, and when he invited her to get out of the car to take in the view she was hesitant. "It's too cold to get out. I'm wearing a dress and it's windy."

Estevan coaxed Kayla to get out to take in the sight. Reluctantly she complied. Kayla recalled Estevan talking about the beauty of the scenery and her beauty. All the while she was thinking, *Couldn't we have had this conversation inside the warm car?*

But when Estevan got down on one knee and pulled out a jewelry box, Kayla couldn't believe he was proposing to her! He put the ring on her finger, as she proclaimed "Yes!" without even looking at the ring. After tears and hugs and kisses, Estevan finally had to remind Kayla to look at her ring for the first time. And of course she loved it!

Estevan had carefully planned every detail of their special day. He even hired a photographer to take pictures of the proposal. But when the photographer texted Estevan that he was stuck in traffic, he figured the event had gone undocumented. Moments later a woman approached them and said, "Hi. I don't mean to intrude on your moment, but I'm a photographer, and I couldn't help but take pictures of you as you got engaged. I would love to email you the photographs as a gift." They were delighted!

Six months later Estevan and Kayla married. What a wonderful wedding they had! All through the day Steve and I rejoiced in the love God had put in their hearts. We marveled at how long they had honored Christ with their purity and how deeply their love for Him spilled over into their love for each other.

## THEN COMES THE BABY...NOT IN THE CARRIAGE

Marriage was better than Estevan and Kayla even imagined. For several years they enjoyed taking romantic getaways and building their lives together. Finally, they decided it was time to have a baby.

When Kayla became pregnant they were both elated. Having a baby was the answer to their prayers. As Kayla's tummy grew, so did their excitement to become parents. Cute maternity clothes, nursery décor, and baby paraphernalia became the topics of their conversations as the two counted down the days.

One day Estevan took Kayla for a routine ultrasound, only to learn the baby no longer had a heartbeat. With no warning their little one had died in Kayla's womb. The doctor could offer no explanation for the loss, but assured them they could try again soon for another baby.

Finding little comfort in the doctor's assurance that they could "try again soon," they went home to wait for Kayla to miscarry. The waiting turned into weeks. The two tried to continue with their responsibilities, but Kayla carrying their dead baby in her womb was a constant reminder of their sorrow. As the days dragged on, waiting for the baby to pass was almost unbearable.

Kayla looked to Estevan to guide her through their loss. And Estevan looked to Christ to give him the strength to do so. Estevan had found strength in God's Word when he lost his mother, and he knew prayer and meditating on Scripture would be what would carry them through now.

When Kayla finally miscarried she hemorrhaged and had to be rushed to the hospital. The heartbreak of the loss, the fear about Kayla's hemorrhaging, and the season after the miscarriage knit Kayla and Estevan's hearts together for a deeper love than they had ever known. And their love for the Lord grew profoundly as well.

The foundation in Christ that Kayla and Estevan had built in their relationship was what carried them through their sorrow. They ached over not being able to hold their little one in their arms, but they celebrated his or her entrance into God's kingdom. That Christmas Estevan and Kayla sent out a Christmas card to help others understand their story. The card read,

> After five months of trying, we were able to conceive. We were thankful to have had the opportunity to hear our sweet baby's heartbeat twice when at Kayla's twelve-week checkup we were unable to locate the heartbeat and learned our baby had stopped growing. We were shocked and very sad, but the Lord gave us such a peace and joy through the whole process. We are so encouraged by the fact that our

baby is with our Lord. Our end goal as parents is that each of our children comes to know and love God and accept salvation in the Lord Jesus Christ. So this just means that our little one has bypassed all of that and is directly in the presence of our Lord. We were so overwhelmed by the love and support of our family and church family through the entire process. The Lord has revealed so much to us about His character through this. He has taught us to trust Him more and to have more of an eternal perspective.

God has been so gracious to us. We also started helping with college ministry in our church and we are loving it! Such a great group that really wants to know Truth. We are praying the Lord would use us to spread the gospel to more people in this age group in our town.

Overall this year has been such an encouraging, exciting, growing, trying, blessed and peaceful time. Our marriage has been built up in Christ.

One year later God blessed Kayla and Estevan with a bouncing baby girl named Everly. And a year after that He gave them yet another baby girl named McKenzie. These days Estevan is the college pastor for our church. The students watched firsthand as Kayla and Estevan glorified Christ through their blessings and trials. And God is using their love for Scripture and wisdom to guide many young men and women to build their own dating relationships on a godly foundation as well.

## PONDER THIS

Kayla and Estevan's story reminds us how deeply young people can care for one another. And although our culture says sex before marriage is inevitable for teens, God can give them strength to walk in obedience to His plan to wait for marriage.

Purity is something for which we must fight. Both young adults as well as their parents must battle *not* against one another, but against the Enemy, who wants to steal, kill, and destroy God's plans for their lives (John 10:10; Ephesians 6:12).

> *Learning to trust God's ways above your own*
> *immediate desires will be the lifeline that leads*
> *you down the path He has planned for you.*

Learning to trust God's ways above your own immediate desires will be the lifeline that leads you down the path He has planned for you. Whether you're a single teen or adult, God's ways are always best, and He promises His blessing for those who obey His commands (Psalm 119:1-3).

## ASK YOURSELF

In your fight to keep your kids from trouble, have you been treating them or their "significant others" as the enemy? You would do well to remember your battle is against Satan's schemes to steal from your kids—and this generation—the life God would have them live in relationship to His Son.

Ephesians 6:12 says, "For we do not wrestle against flesh and blood, but against principalities, against powers, against the rulers of the darkness of this world, against spiritual wickedness in high places" (KJV).

Learning to guide your kids through their dating years is not for the faint of heart. As with any ministry to which God calls you, as a parent it is vital that you seek His wisdom daily through Bible study, prayer, and godly counsel.

## 22

# She Feels Like Home

### Brandon and Jessy

Our son Brandon was a junior in college and still had not met anyone he was interested in dating. While enjoying his passion to study music, he kept one eye out as he prayed for God to direct him to someone with whom he could spend the rest of his life.

By the middle of that year, Brandon was busy with his studies and interning at a nearby church as a worship leader for their college group. He also regularly played worship for their youth department.

Brandon recalled, "When I went to play worship for the youth, I had my blinders on. I was there to minister and did not want to be distracted by the attention I might receive from any of the young girls."

Jessy remembered being a senior in high school when she first noticed Brandon. She was in the youth group where Brandon played drums for worship. All her friends thought he was cute, and she did too. Jessy was keenly aware of Brandon, although he had not noticed her at all. "I saw him on stage each week. I remember thinking he had really nice arms," Jessy said, laughing.

At the time Jessy was interested in another boy, so she didn't give much thought to the guy with the nice arms.

That summer Jessy attended youth camp, and it just so happened that Brandon also went there to play worship. Brandon remembers, "The first time I became aware of Jessy was when she got hurt at camp.

She fell on the AstroTurf during recreation and badly scraped her knees."

As the youth leaders talked about the girl who got hurt, Brandon learned Jessy's name. He also discovered that the cute girl with the banged-up knees was a high school graduate. "That's when my blinders came off, because she was now an adult. And that's when I thought, *Jessy is really cute*," Brandon said, laughing.

Brandon began to observe Jessy with her friends to see what kind of person she was. He noticed she was part of the "in crowd," yet popularity didn't make Jessy self-absorbed or conceited. Quite the opposite was true. She was comfortable with her friends as well as welcoming to others outside their group, a trait Brandon quickly admired.

That summer the college group where Brandon was a leader put on their annual beach trip to welcome incoming high school graduates. Far more young graduates were at the event than the regular group of older college students. Brandon felt a bit out of place since he was so much older than most of the students. However, he was in leadership, so he stepped out of his comfort zone and jumped into a car full of young people.

Fortunately, another college leader was driving the car so Brandon wasn't the only one in the vehicle who was older. Brandon happened to sit in the back next to Jessy, but feeling rather awkward among the younger crowd, he distracted himself with his phone.

Jessy thought, *Why is this guy so focused on his phone?*

On the ride to the beach, the other college leader asked everyone thought-provoking questions. Without looking up from his phone, Brandon listened intently to Jessy's answers about her views on life and spiritual matters. He was impressed with her depth and thoughtfulness. Her discerning responses intrigued Brandon, and he wanted to get to know her better.

Jessy also listened carefully to how Brandon answered the questions. She liked hearing him share, because it gave her a glimpse into the person he really was. Up to that point Jessy knew Brandon to be quiet and reserved, so having an opportunity to learn more about him sparked her interest in him.

## MIXED SIGNALS

That fall Brandon began his senior year of college at California Baptist University, and all his spare time was spent interning at church. Brandon had gone to school to study music and Bible with the intention of one day becoming a worship pastor, so interning at the church was a great training opportunity. Although, after graduation, Brandon's goal was to first enjoy a season of touring and playing with some Christian bands before he settled into a church ministry.

Jessy had also started working for their church in the counseling department. At work Brandon began looking for reasons to walk by her desk. Whenever he did, he tried to think of clever ways to strike up a conversation with her. As time went on their chats became more comfortable and more frequent, until each secretly looked forward to opportunities to talk.

At college group the two kept one eye on each other. Often their eyes would meet across the room and they would smile. As Jessy interacted with others there, Brandon observed how she and another guy she had once dated seemed to still be interested in each other, so Brandon didn't make a move toward dating Jessy.

Jessy was over the boy, but she didn't know how to let Brandon know. At one point she "asked Brandon's advice" about what she should do to let a particular young man know she was not interested in dating him without being rude. Laughing, Jessy told me, "I was hoping to subtly let Brandon know I was not interested in the guy. I was new to dating and trying to figure it all out."

Then Brandon noticed a friend of his seemed to be interested in Jessy. He watched to see what would come of that, but then he finally asked the friend about his intentions. When Brandon's buddy said he wasn't going to pursue Jessy, he decided it was time to ask her out.

Jessy was looking for ways to show Brandon she wanted him to ask her out. One night after church she slipped off her high heels and waited around until everyone else started to leave. She hung back in her bare feet, hoping Brandon would come up and talk to her, and he did. Jessy recalled, "I took off my shoes because I was worried my height might have put him off."

Before Brandon had made the move to ask Jessy out, they found themselves attending their church's fall festival, where Brandon's job was to sit in the dunk tank all night. Brandon thought, *It's kind of hard to ask a girl on a date when you're spending the entire evening in a dunk tank.*

Afterward Brandon was trying to welcome a girl he knew from school to the college group, but then he was concerned he might be giving Jessy the idea that he liked the girl. He confided in Jessy that he may have given the college girl the wrong impression, so he asked for her help by going with them to grab a bite to eat. Jessy was still trying to figure out if Brandon had feelings for her or if he was just reaching out to her as a friend.

## A COFFEE DATE

Finally, Brandon called Jessy and asked her out to coffee—just the two of them. It was late, so they met at an IHOP. Nothing else was open. Jessy was so excited to be alone with Brandon. She recalled, "As Brandon talked, I was trying to play it cool, but I couldn't stop smiling."

Both laughed when they realized they had been misreading each other's signals and holding back when they thought the other wasn't interested.

Brandon and Jessy dated each other exclusively for the rest of the school year. They had a lot of fun together, and they grew to deeply care for each other. But their relationship was not without conflict. Jessy recalled, "We each had high expectations of the other and were lacking in selflessness."

When Brandon graduated he was offered an opportunity in another city to pursue his passion for a career in music. He was torn because he really did care for Jessy, but he was unwilling to give up his goals to have a relationship with her. Brandon knew other musicians who had regretted getting married before they pursued their dreams, and he was wary of making the same mistake.

Two weeks before Brandon left town he broke up with Jessy, explaining that he didn't want to be tied down to a long-distance relationship. He wanted to focus on his opportunity. Jessy was devastated, and Brandon was too.

For the next two weeks Brandon still saw Jessy at church and even went to Disneyland with her on her birthday because they had already planned to do so. Brandon said, "I still really cared about her. When we said good-bye I wanted to kiss her, but I didn't."

Jessy added, "I thought he was gonna kiss me good-bye. I wanted him to, but he didn't. Which I see now would only have been more confusing for me."

## DON'T LOOK BACK

Brandon left for his new life and tried not to look back. He wrapped himself up in music and touring and tried to enjoy living the life he had always dreamed of. But something was missing.

While his opportunities to play with some awesome Christian bands should have been enough, his heart ached to share his experience with Jessy.

After many months of no contact, Jessy wrote Brandon a letter to explain how she was feeling. She still cared for him and thought he cared for her too. But if he was truly done, she needed closure.

Jessy recalled, "Brandon didn't respond at all. I was really disappointed in him for not responding. But then I thought maybe this was what I needed to know, that he was really over me, so I could move on."

Brandon said, "When I got her letter I thought, *How am I going to respond to this?* I still cared about her a lot. So I procrastinated."

Not long after receiving the letter, Brandon also received a kind and gentle nudge from Jessy's mom to at least respond to her daughter's note because she was really hurting.

Brandon messaged Jessy. "I just haven't known what to say. There is no one else I am interested in. You're the one I am thinking of. No one compares to you. Everyone and everything else is black-and-white and you're in color."

After that the two talked on the phone. Jessy asked Brandon, "Why are we not together? We have had a great time apart, but we are still hung up on each other. Why don't we give it another try?"

With that Brandon jumped into his car and drove six hours into the night to see Jessy. She could hardly believe it when he arrived on her doorstep. And she was overjoyed to hear Brandon say he wanted them to be a couple again!

## HOME

As a mother, watching your son fall in love is a wonderful experience. And yet it is also a season of quietly asking God to grant him wisdom and discernment to find the wife who will love him deeply and help him pursue Christ.

*Watching your son fall in love
is a wonderful experience.*

When Brandon and Jessy were falling in love, we lived several hours away, so most of what my husband and I knew of Jessy and their relationship came from conversations with Brandon. His love for her was evident from the start. While he talked about how he was wrestling with wanting to pursue his dreams as a single man yet longing to be with Jessy, it wasn't easy to know what advice to give.

But I'll never forget the conversation Brandon and I shared after he and Jessy got back together. I asked my son, "So what is it about Jessy that makes you want to be with her?"

Brandon looked at me and said, "Momma, I have been living my dream. Touring with some pretty awesome people and doing some really cool things. And all the while I kept wanting to pick up the phone and share it with Jessy. I knew I couldn't call her when we were apart, but I really wanted to."

Brandon paused, and then went on. "But the day I called Jessy and heard her voice for the first time in so many months, it was like…home."

With that I knew my boy had found the love of his life. I knew God had brought to our son the woman who would make a home with him no matter where the Lord led them.

## FULL CIRCLE

Brandon and Jessy continued in a long-distance relationship while Brandon moved to Nashville to work in the Christian music industry.

After he and Jessy were married in a beautiful ceremony in Southern California, Jessy moved to Nashville too.

After a time in Tennessee, Brandon came to realize his dream to tour as a musician paled against his dream to be home with Jessy each night. God also worked in Brandon to develop a heart to minister in the local church.

As Brandon and Jessy prayed and waited on God, He brought them through some refining fires that only knit their hearts closer to Christ— and to each other.

On the day the church where Brandon and Jessy had met called to offer Brandon a job as worship leader, the couple could hardly believe the Lord's kindness to them. Moving back to California to minister in the very church where they fell in love was beyond what they could have hoped for. God not only gave Brandon his dream of marrying the love of his life, but He brought Brandon and Jessy full circle to where their hearts had been all along. And God's blessings continue as the couple just had their first child—a baby boy named Ledger Brandon.

## PONDER THIS

Observing God knit together two hearts in love, for Him and for each other, is glorious. To finally meet Jessy and see how she so complemented our son after my years of praying and waiting for God to bring him a godly wife was glorious!

Do you realize the Lord is more interested in directing your children toward godly spouses than you are in helping them find one? But before God will lead them to love another, He wants them to learn how to love Him with their whole heart. When a person's love for God is the priority of their life, their love for their spouse will be selfless and Christ-honoring as well.

By teaching your children how they can trust God's character and love for them from Scripture, you will equip them to look to their heavenly Father for guidance as they look for a spouse.

Genesis 24 is a wonderful insight into how God carefully led

Abraham's servant to find the wife He intended for Isaac. These days we parents can't go fetch a spouse for our kids, but we can learn from Abraham's example to trust God and prayerfully wait for the Lord to providentially provide.

## ASK YOURSELF

Are you the mother of a son looking for love? Or maybe your daughter has been wounded by some punk who chose to follow his dreams over a relationship with her. How you handle those situations as a parent is vitally important.

In the years my husband and I have been in ministry, we've watched moms (and sometimes dads) step into the drama of their young adults' dating lives, only to wreak havoc.

*Ask God to give you His wisdom for how He would have you guide your child through the confusing waters of dating and courtship.*

You would do well to remember that overstepping your place as a parent could end up wounding the very person your child ends up marrying. Take a step back and ask God to give you His wisdom for how He would have you guide your child through the confusing waters of dating and courtship. Offering godly counsel based on biblical principles is a great place to start.

And if you're the one looking for love, keep trusting God for His perfect plan. It's all about where you fix your gaze. The more you press into your love for Jesus, the more He will satisfy and direct the longings of your heart. Take to heart the advice from Hebrews 12:2: "Looking unto Jesus, the author and finisher of our faith."

## 23

# Turning To Each Other in Trial

## Jake and Meredith

J ake played high school football and baseball near Seattle, Washington. He knew he was eligible for some baseball scholarships at local colleges, but he had his sights set on attending a Christian college in Southern California. The private school tuition was rather steep, but the restaurant where Jake worked in Washington had a franchise near the college in Southern California, and he hoped he would be able to pay his tuition by transferring to that location. The plan seemed perfect. After filling out all the application forms, Jake waited to hear if he would be accepted.

The time Jake expected to receive an acceptance letter came and went, but he continued to hope and pray God would make a way for him to attend the college in Southern California. When summer drew to a close and he still had not heard from the school, he started to lose hope. When the start date for freshman orientation passed, Jake began to look for other options. But then one week later he finally received that acceptance letter.

For some the idea of a last-minute response to such a letter would be out of the question. But Jake didn't hesitate to jump at the opportunity. After throwing a few things in his car and kissing his family goodbye, Jake drove off to a new life.

Although he was an excellent pitcher and was well prepared to play college baseball, he hadn't been offered any athletic scholarships. But he didn't let that hold him back. As he drove toward school, he left the details of how he would pay his tuition in God's hands.

After Jake arrived and settled in, Jake's dad, Brent, called to tell him how important it was to him that Jake try out for the college team. He didn't want Jake to miss out on the opportunity to play college baseball, and he was planning to take on extra work to pay for Jake's tuition so he wouldn't need to work at the restaurant.

At first Jake was reluctant to accept his father's generous offer. But in response to Brent's convincing influence, Jake finally agreed to his proposal.

As the Lord would have it, and to Jake's excitement, when he went out for the baseball team he was offered a scholarship for playing, along with a part-time job on campus that alleviated some of the financial pressure on Brent.

## THE TALL FUNNY GUY

Our oldest daughter, Meredith, was a junior in college when she met Jake. She loved school, loved her friends, and was looking forward to following the Lord wherever He might lead her after graduation. While she was not necessarily looking for a husband, she couldn't help but notice the new student, Jake. He was a handsome young man who seemed to make everybody laugh.

Meredith and Jake became friends with the same people, so they enjoyed a lot of time together. Meredith loved to laugh, and Jake's humor appealed to her. Jake was drawn to the blonde with the laugh that lit up a room.

Yet the more Jake worked to get Meredith's attention, the less interested in him she seemed to be. The worst memory Jake recalled was when, in an attempt to be funny, he jumped up on a table in the cafeteria while impersonating a dinosaur, specifically a velociraptor. Several friends had gathered around, laughing hysterically at Jake's antics. Meredith walked into the cafeteria and looked over at the commotion in Jake's direction. Just as his eyes met hers, the table gave way. Jake toppled to the floor, and the whole room erupted in laughter.

Meredith was embarrassed for poor Jake, so she quickly looked away and walked back out of the cafeteria, pretending not to have seen his fall.

One Valentine's Day Jake made a cute little card for Meredith to test the waters. The card was innocent enough, saying, "Roses are red, violets are blue. I don't know, but I think I like you." But for Meredith, who was unsure of how she felt about Jake, it was too close to asking her to commit to a relationship She ran the other way.

## HE HARDENED HIS HEART

Since Meredith seemed uninterested, Jake felt free to date other girls. When he finally, as he put it, "hardened his heart" toward her, he thought he could get serious about looking for someone else. But then Meredith appeared to become interested in Jake as more than a friend.

One night while coming back from an outing with a group of friends, Meredith sat next to Jake in the car and fell asleep on his shoulder—something she had never done before. Jake was confused, but he decided it was time to talk to Meredith about his feelings for her.

Meredith knew she was sending poor Jake mixed signals. On one hand, she was attracted to him and enjoyed his company. But she had never been one to have a serious boyfriend, and she wasn't sure how she felt about the idea. Meredith had seen friends go from one boyfriend to the next, but that had never been her way. She had "liked" boys from time to time, but when it came to a serious relationship, she was holding out for the one she would give her heart to for the rest of her life—in marriage. In Meredith's mind a decision to date Jake would amount to more than simply dating; it would likely lead her to marriage. The weight of that idea was intimidating.

Soon Meredith began calling home to talk with Steve and me about her feelings for Jake. She wanted our advice as she considered the idea of dating him. When she called crying because she thought she had pushed Jake too far away, Steve and I realized our little girl just might be in love.

The school Meredith and Jake attended was four hours from our home, so we had never met Jake. It's a strange experience to know your daughter is falling for a man you've never met. But Steve and I knew

Meredith was committed to honoring Christ in her relationships, so we prayed for her to have God's wisdom and trusted the Spirit to lead our little girl.

## MEET THE PARENTS

When Meredith began to pray for God to show her what He would have for her and Jake, she became confident that He was leading her to a relationship with him. The next time Jake told Meredith of his feelings for her she was happy to tell him of her feelings for him. Both were elated and ready to begin their relationship. But first Meredith wanted Jake to meet her family. He was a little intimidated when Meredith said, "Before we can date you have to meet my parents and get my father's approval."

Every Easter, Steve and I host an all-church baptism and barbecue at our ranch in Northern California. Usually a couple hundred people attend the event. That year Meredith invited Jake to come home with her for that weekend to meet her family—and particularly to have a talk with her father about dating her.

After driving the four hours from school and then another 45 minutes up a canyon to reach our ranch, Jake was more than ready to get out of the car. It was already dark outside when they pulled up to the house. Meredith and Jake could see me through the kitchen window, standing on a ladder, painting a wall. I was so excited to see them that I threw my arms up in the air and opened my mouth, pretending to scream with excitement. At that very moment, the peacocks who sleep high up in our pine trees began to scream. Jake's eyes got as big as saucers. He turned to Meredith and asked, "Is that your mom screaming that loudly?"

He must have been a bit freaked out to arrive in the middle of nowhere on a very dark night only to be welcomed by a crazy lady standing on a ladder screaming at them. I still can't think of that story without laughing.

When Jake came into the house and Meredith told me what happened, we all had a great laugh together, which broke the ice for our introduction.

Meredith had grown up in our church, so everyone was interested in meeting the tall young man she brought home. At one point during the party, I noticed Jake was seated on the sofa with a half-dozen men circled around him, grilling him with questions. I think they were trying to be subtle, but it was pretty obvious these men who cared for Meredith were not gonna let just any old guy date her. When Steve's good friend, John, looked over, acted like he was scratching his nose with his thumb, and subtly gave Steve a "thumbs-up," we had to laugh. Jake knew exactly what was going on.

After the scrutiny of Meredith's church family, Jake also submitted himself to a one-on-one visit with her father. When Jake told Steve he was seriously considering asking Meredith to be his wife, the two agreed to talk on the phone once a week so Steve could come to know Jake better.

## CANDLES IN THE SAND

By the end of Meredith's senior year, Jake had received Steve's blessing to ask her to be his bride. But Jake was a "starving student," and he had little money to buy a ring with a diamond. When he informed us Meredith said she would be happy with a simple band as an engagement ring, I pulled Jake aside to offer him one of my diamonds. I said, "Jake, I don't mean to overstep, and I am not a mom who thinks it's vital for my daughter to have a diamond in her engagement ring. But if it wouldn't offend you, I'd love to offer you the diamond in the necklace Steve gave me when Meredith was born."

Pride is destructive in a marriage relationship, and Jake's grateful response only served to assure us that he would love our daughter with kindness and humility. His reply made us love him even more when he said, "Oh wow! I think that would be great. I really want Mer to have a diamond in her ring. And it makes it even more special that Steve gave you the diamond when you gave birth to Meredith."

Jake kept the proposal a secret from our daughter until he took her on a date to the beach one night. As they walked barefoot along the water's edge, they came upon lit candles arranged in the shape of a heart in the sand. And scattered in the heart were rose petals. Jake's friends had secretly gone ahead of them to set up the lovely spot. When the couple approached, rather than finding the scene romantic, Meredith was a bit freaked out. "Jake, this looks like a seance! Let's get out of here!"

Jake laughed and led her by the hand toward the candles. He got down on one knee, and as he opened the jewelry box to show Meredith the ring, he asked her to be his bride.

Meredith hugged Jake tightly and said, "Yes!"

After the two lingered at the beach, talking of their hopes and dreams, they headed back to the college to announce their engagement. Jake had given Meredith's friends a heads-up, so when they arrived back at school the couple was met with a surprise engagement party!

Jake's parents met Meredith for the first time at her college graduation. Jake was close to his parents and had been talking with them throughout his and Meredith's relationship, so they were excited to finally meet her.

I happened to be videotaping Meredith in her cap and gown as Jake brought his parents to introduce them to her. I was able to capture these wonderful people scooping Meredith into their arms and offering her their love and support. I was moved to tears when Brent looked to his wife, Gloria, and said, "There she is, Glor! There's the one we have been praying for God to send to Jake since the day he was born." And I captured *that* on video too! (Anyone else need a tissue?)

## A GARDEN WEDDING

Jake and Meredith were married in a beautiful garden wedding on an incredibly hot July evening. Jake's siblings and some of his groomsmen were from Seattle, so the 100-degree California Central Valley heat was nearly too much for them. After a night of celebrating under a full moon, the two sped off to enjoy a romantic honeymoon at an all-inclusive resort in Mexico.

Their first hitch as husband and wife came only one day after the wedding. Jake realized he'd booked Meredith's travel in her new married name, but all her identification still carried her maiden name. Jake stepped up to resolve the issue, and after many phone calls and with only moments to spare before their flight left, a notary met them at the ticket counter to verify their marriage license and Meredith's name change.

After their honeymoon, they moved three hours north of us to find jobs and volunteer to work alongside a friend there in youth ministry. The little house they rented ended up having a terrible mold issue that caused Meredith to struggle with respiratory issues for the entire year they lived there. At the landlord's suggestion Meredith would wipe down the walls with bleach, only to have it reappear with a vengeance. Working long hours, volunteering in ministry, and trying to keep up with the mold was certainly a time of refining for their marriage.

## BACK WHERE THEY STARTED

A year later, when Meredith's father shattered his hip in a motor-cycle accident, they dropped everything to move back home to help us out on the ranch. While it was a fun season for the two to be living near family, about a year later Meredith couldn't turn down a job offer to work back at the college where she and Jake first met.

Her position as a resident director at The Master's University allowed them to live on campus and gave Jake the opportunity to finish his degree. Then after two years, Meredith and Jake spent a summer backpacking through Europe, where she became pregnant with their first child. Upon learning she was pregnant and would likely take leave from her job mid-semester, the school offered Jake an RD position, which helped him to continue his education at the seminary.

Life was busy and fun for Jake and Meredith. Living in an apartment in the middle of a guys' dormitory meant never a dull moment. Their daughter, Karis, naturally became the princess of the dorm. As you can imagine, she grew up with many "loyal subjects," who entertained her as she dressed up like royalty each day.

When Karis was two years old, Jake and Meredith were overjoyed to be pregnant with their second child. But their joy was soon replaced with sorrow when their doctor informed them the pregnancy was ecto-pic. Learning the baby was not in Meredith's uterus but rather in her fallopian tube wasn't easy news to process. They questioned the doctor, "Is the baby alive? What can we do to save it? What's our next step?"

When the doctor explained that an ectopic pregnancy could kill Meredith and the baby had no hope of surviving, he rather passively told them to eliminate the pregnancy. But Meredith and Jake wanted to be sure the mass the ultrasound showed in the fallopian tube was indeed the baby and not some sort of tumor the tech may have mistaken for their baby. When a 4D ultrasound revealed the baby was indeed in the tube and no longer alive, they were relieved they didn't have to make a decision to terminate the pregnancy.

## I'LL HOLD YOU IN HEAVEN

Karis had been excited about the idea of a new sibling. Through the many days her parents were processing their loss, she could tell something was wrong. When Jake and Meredith finally sat down to explain the baby had died, Karis brought her little hands up to her face to cry in them. When she stopped, she looked into Meredith's eyes and put one hand on each of her shoulders. "It's okay, Mommy," she said. "You will hold it in heaven."

With that, Meredith, Jake, and Karis all had a good cry as they celebrated the idea that one day they would meet their baby in heaven. Through their loss Meredith and Jake pressed into their love for Christ and for each other.

That same year Jake's brother died in a motorcycle accident. Jake was close to his brother, and the loss was heartbreaking to him and the rest of his family. The funeral was well attended by people Jake and his siblings had gone to school with. Jake's deep grief was overshadowed with hope when God granted him the privilege of delivering the message of salvation at the funeral. He prayed for God to use their hope in Christ amid their grief to bring many of their friends to the Lord.

All the while, Jake was trying to finish seminary classes, work as a college RD, and spend time with his wife and daughter. As he struggled through a season of deep sorrow over the loss of his brother, Meredith devoted herself to praying for Jake and looking for ways to encourage him and help him with his heavy load.

After the ectopic pregnancy, Meredith had another miscarriage. When she got pregnant again and carried the baby full term, they were overjoyed. Meredith's sister, Kayla, had also experienced a miscarriage during this time, so the whole family was beyond excited to greet little Ivy Love on the night she was born.

As the family converged upon the delivery room to meet the new baby, Jake stopped us at the door to explain that Ivy had been born with some unexpected craniofacial deformities. In that moment, everything changed. Our elation turned to concern and our concern to confusion as the doctors examined sweet little Ivy.

Meredith had only gotten a glimpse at Ivy as she was laid on her chest moments after she was born. When I walked into the room, *my* daughter, Meredith, was lying in the bed where she had just delivered. Quietly she was repeating over and over, "I want my baby." Ivy was being examined in the same room just out of Meredith's line of sight.

As Ivy cried while being poked and prodded, I walked over and held her tiny hand. When I sang in her little ear, "Jesus loves me, this I know," she quieted and seemed to be comforted by my singing.

The next few hours were filled with specialists and doctors assessing Ivy's condition. At one point she failed her hearing test and they said she might be deaf. But this grandmother remembered her quieting at my singing, so I had hope the test was wrong. All night we prayed for God to grant Ivy the gift of hearing. Our son, Brandon, a musician, stayed up all night, pleading with God to allow Ivy the ability to hear music.

When Ivy passed her hearing test the next day, we all wept with relief and rejoiced in God's goodness. As the days went on the doctors diagnosed her with a rare syndrome called Goldenhar. Thankfully, Ivy's case was less severe than it could have been, but she would still be facing several surgeries, physical therapy, and other procedures.

Through the experience, Jake and Meredith were held up by their faith in Christ and in His love for them—and for Ivy. One day Meredith said to me, "Mom, this is Ivy's trial. God is entrusting us to prepare her to walk through it with her eyes on Him."

Not long after Ivy's birth, Meredith became pregnant with twins.

The beautiful truth of Job 1:21—"The Lᴏʀᴅ gave, and the Lᴏʀᴅ has taken away; Blessed be the name of the Lᴏʀᴅ"—rang in my heart at the wonderful news of God's blessing them with not one but two babies. But our elation was short-lived. After several months, an ultrasound revealed the twins no longer had heartbeats. Again, I tearfully recited in my mind, *The Lᴏʀᴅ gave, and the Lᴏʀᴅ has taken away; Blessed be the name of the Lᴏʀᴅ.*

## WORTHY TO SUFFER

As Steve and I observed Jake and Meredith honor Christ in their trial, one scripture kept rolling over in my mind. Acts 5:41 says the apostles were "rejoicing that they were counted worthy to suffer."

What an incredible perspective Meredith and Jake had. As others offered their all-too-common "Christian pat answers" about why God would allow their circumstance, they found great comfort in not needing to know the answers. Knowing that God loved them, ordained that Ivy would be born to them, and that He promised to grant them His grace to daily meet their daughter's needs was enough for them.

Since Meredith was unable to nurse Ivy because of her cleft lip and pallet, she pumped her breast milk for an entire year so she could give Ivy her milk through a special bottle.

When a specialist informed them Ivy's first surgery needed to be redone because it had been unsuccessful, again they looked to God for His grace and peace.

All the while, Jake and Meredith were still living in the RD's apartment on the college campus. Through their example the students watched firsthand what it looked like to trust God when life doesn't turn out the way you planned.

Ivy has had four major surgeries in her short lifetime, and she will face many more. But God has abundantly provided amazing specialists. By His providence, the leading specialist in Goldenhar syndrome happened to work within an hour's drive of where Jake and Meredith were living. And when insurance wouldn't cover the specialist, they prayed for help and God made a way.

## GOD'S PLAN ALL ALONG

Unforeseen trials undermine many marriages. But Jake and Meredith saw how God brought the two of them together for this ministry to Ivy. The Lord had graciously prepared them ahead of time as they learned His character through the study of Scripture. Sound teaching from their pastors and college professors had equipped both Meredith and Jake for the difficult season. They learned to lean on each other for strength, but more importantly they prayed together for God to grant them His peace, wisdom, and even joy as they became advocates for Ivy's health issues.

Big sister Karis is Ivy's closest friend. She's always ready to hold her hand and offer encouragement whenever she has to visit the doctor or face another surgical procedure. God has recently blessed Jake and Meredith with yet another baby girl, named Eliza, and Ivy is now an adorable, delightful two-year-old. Her spitfire attitude and beautiful smile lights up any room. With her little pink glasses and her sassy little ways, she is truly a treasure given by God.

With each surgery Ivy has faced, Jake and Meredith have continued to look to God for His wisdom, strength, and grace. Sure, it's a scary experience to watch your baby endure major surgeries and anesthesia, but knowing that God's love for Ivy far exceeds their love for her gives Jake and Meredith His peace. They know they can trust Him to cause all things to work together for good for them and for sweet Ivy Love.

## PONDER THIS

When Jake and Meredith were young college students, God answered their parents' prayers by drawing them together. In His providence and provision, He knit their hearts together in love for Christ and for each other. God used Jake and Meredith to minister to countless college students, while He also equipped them to walk together through difficult times. Rather than turning away from God or from each other, their unforeseen trials caused them to look to the Lord for wisdom and strength.

*In His providence and provision, He knit their hearts together in love for Christ and for each other.*

Spending time knowing Jesus through prayer and studying His Word will prepare you to trust Him when unexpected trouble comes. And when you realize He loves your children even more than you do, you can rest in knowing they are the apple of His eye and you can trust Him with their well-being. Pray this psalm over your children, and then rest in knowing God's love and care for them far exceeds your own.

Keep me as the apple of your eye;
hide me in the shadow of your wings.
Psalm 17:8 ESV

## ASK YOURSELF

*The secret to building a marriage that will withstand the trying times of life is to know and love God so intimately that you'll recognize how anything that comes across your path is filtered through His loving hands.*

Are you preparing your children to find godly spouses? Are you asking God to bring your kids spouses to encourage them in their walk with Christ? When your kids dream of marriage, do more than let them talk about how finding "the right one" will make them happy. Teach them that the priority of life is to find their happiness and worth in a relationship with their creator. When they understand how dearly they are loved by God, they will be less likely to look for their worth in how a spouse might treat them.

Looking to another person to fill the void only God can fill is idolatry—plain and simple. The secret to building a marriage that will withstand the trying times of life is to know and love God so intimately that you'll recognize how anything that comes across your path is filtered through His loving hands. Only He can work all things together for good for you and your children (Romans 8:28).

## 24

# The Surprise Wedding

## Tony and Kylene

God did not bring our oldest son, Tony, to our family until he was 15 years old. In more than a decade of youth ministry, my husband and I had met numerous kids who would benefit from the security of living with us, but until we met Tony God had never led us to take any of them into our home.

When we met Tony he had just given his heart to Christ. He was attending the church where my husband, Steve, had recently accepted a position as youth pastor. The day I introduced myself to Tony he had a bandage on his hand. He had somehow cut it deeply, and rather than going to a doctor, he had treated the injury himself. I couldn't help but mother him, so I asked to see the cut. I was impressed with the remarkable job he'd done to dress the wound.

Tony was the kind of kid everyone loved. He was quite handsome with his dark-brown hair and bright blue eyes. No one ever would have guessed he was going through such a difficult time. (You can read more about how Tony came to be our son in my book *Moms Raising Sons to Be Men*.)

The more Tony grew in his walk with the Lord, the more time he spent at our home. It didn't take long to see how his good looks and charm were a magnet for the girls in our youth group. Steve took Tony under his wing and began to mentor him in his walk with Christ. He showed him how God expects His followers to honor Him in their dating lives, as well as in all aspects of character.

After a series of events in Tony's life, Steve and I believed it was time for him to move in with our family. We all loved Tony dearly, and we were all in agreement that the Lord would have us take him in. After Steve invited Tony to move in with us, he also proceeded to outline the "rules of the house" and the expectations he would have of him as the eldest son. Tony could hardly believe he'd been welcomed into our family, and he was more than happy to comply with Steve's stipulations.

As Tony settled in we couldn't have been happier with the situation. He was respectful, kind, and a wonderful addition to the Stoppe household. Watching him observe Steve to learn how a godly man loves and honors his family is by far one of my favorite memories of Tony's early days at home. As Tony put it, "The family was, and continues to be, my living definition of both what God expects from me, and what He wants for me. I am thankful for this example, and I have no doubt that it was God's plan for our lives to connect."

## THE DATING GAME

Along with our new son came quite a bit of activity in the dating department. Our phone rang off the hook with calls from girls (this was back before teenagers all had cell phones). Looking for ways to have mother-son talks with Tony about how to honor the opposite sex meant I spent many warm Texas nights seated in his Jeep while he worked on its engine.

My heart was to help Tony realize the importance of walking in purity to allow the Holy Spirit to guide him in choosing a godly wife. While my words were not wasted on Tony, it would be several years before they would truly have an influence on him.

*My heart was to help Tony realize the importance*
*of walking in purity to allow the Holy Spirit to*
*guide him in choosing a godly wife.*

Tony played football, was senior class president, and was named valedictorian of his graduating class. At his graduation, everyone cheered when Tony walked across the stage, received his diploma, and then joyfully picked up and spun around the tiny woman principal.

Steve and I could not have been more proud of his accomplishments. Yet we were even more proud of how the Lord was slowly transforming our boy into a man with a heart for God.

After high school Tony went to Texas A&M University, which was a couple of hours away from our home in Lakeway, Texas. With his sights set on becoming a fighter pilot, he worked hard at school and in the ROTC program at A&M. When Tony graduated, he was granted a fighter pilot slot in the United States Air Force.

When Tony arrived in Panama City, Florida, for flight training, he was living the dream he'd had since he was a boy. But somehow "having it all" didn't seem enough for Tony.

One day he called home to tell us about his amazing experiences as a jet pilot. After much technical fly-boy talk, he changed the subject. "I've been attending church off base where my Sunday school teacher is a retired fighter pilot. He said something that really impacted me. He said, 'You know, if God allowed you to be a fighter pilot, it's not because you're all that. Rather, God has chosen you for this job to bring glory to Christ.'"

With that statement, the Holy Spirit grabbed hold of Tony in a fresh way and began to guide his thinking with a biblical perspective. As Tony advanced in his training, we also observed great strides in his spiritual growth as he sat under the teaching of the retired fighter pilot. And when Tony began telling us about a beautiful girl he met on the beach in Panama City, we were intrigued that the Lord might indeed be leading him to the one he would marry.

## THAT FEISTY SOUTHERN GIRL

Kylene was raised on the beaches of Florida, and she'd watched many of her girlfriends set their sights on the fighter pilots who came through their community during training. She also observed how these girls would do just about anything to hook themselves a pilot. Kylene was not such a girl.

Kylene was in nursing school and was working hard to finish her degree. She was a Christian, and she had recently made a commitment to seek the Lord for His guidance in both her career and dating relationships.

Looking for a husband was not on her agenda one day as she played volleyball with her friends on the beach. But a young fighter pilot in training asked her on a date, and she agreed. Then on the date Kylene realized he was more interested in a one-night stand than in getting to know her as a person. She was furious and immediately put an end to their evening.

When the fighter pilot later shared with Tony his frustration over the lack of cooperation from the feisty young girl with the heavy Georgian accent, Tony was intrigued.

Days later, when Tony saw Kylene on the beach playing volleyball, he made it a point to introduce himself. As they spent time together on the beach, Tony was impressed that Kylene wasn't like other girls who would shamelessly throw themselves at the pilots. He thought, *She has a good head on her shoulders.* He also respected her determination to not have sex until marriage.

With the day of Tony's new assignment and inevitable move away from Florida fast approaching, the two spent more and more time together. Tony knew he was just beginning his career as a fighter pilot, so he tried to put the idea of marriage out of his mind. On the day they were to part, the two agreed to keep in touch, but there was no talk of "forever."

## NOT READY FOR MARRIAGE

Tony left Florida in February, and before leaving for his next assignment in Okinawa, Japan, he came home to see us in California, where we had recently relocated. Tony talked about all the exciting details that go along with learning to fly fighter jets. But he also talked a lot about Kylene, that beautiful southern girl he'd met in Florida. He was careful to remind us, "I'm not ready to get married. I need to focus on my career." But we could see Kylene had affected him differently from any other girl. This girl had captured the heart of our boy.

Several months later Tony began making plans to come home from

Japan for Thanksgiving. One night he called and asked if it would be all right if Kylene came to our home for the holiday as well. He assured us, "I just want her to meet the family. I'm not gonna get married or anything. But I want y'all to meet her and let me know what you think."

Of course, we agreed. The whole family was excited for an opportunity to meet the girl who had stolen Tony's heart. A couple of months before they were scheduled to come, Tony called again. This time there was a sense of urgency in his voice as he explained. "You know, I was lying in my bed this morning, thinking about Kylene. And all of a sudden I thought to myself, *I'm gonna marry that girl.* And now that's all I can think about! So what I'd like to do is propose to her when she comes for the visit."

Steve and I couldn't have been happier to hear Tony explain how he had been praying about the idea of marrying Kylene and had God's peace that she was the one.

The plan Tony came up with was to surprise Kylene with a ring and a proposal in San Francisco on the day he picked her up from the airport. Then Tony would bring Kylene home to meet the family. Kylene and Tony had not even discussed the idea of him asking her to marry him, so his proposal would come as a complete surprise to her.

The excitement mounted when, two weeks before the couple was to arrive, Tony called home with yet another idea. "So I've been thinking. I really want Kylene to marry me while we're there. So if she says yes to the proposal, I want to surprise her with a quick and quiet ceremony at the house."

Steve is a pastor, so Tony had the idea that, after Thanksgiving dinner, with our immediate family present, Steve could just say a few words over the couple and pronounce them husband and wife. "We can have a quick ceremony like that," he said, "and then later have a real wedding when we have the time and money to plan it."

That's when I took the phone from Steve. "I'm so excited that you've found the woman you love so much you can't wait to marry her. But I'm not as excited about your idea to have a quick wedding in hopes of having a *real* wedding later. I know several military wives who got married quickly, expecting a nice ceremony later. In most cases the wedding they hoped for never came to be."

I went on to encourage Tony to let us put on a nice wedding for them during that visit—*if* Kylene agreed to marry him and *if* she would go along with the idea. I outlined the stipulations to Tony. "If she's going to have a real wedding, then she needs a real wedding dress, you need to get her father's permission, and she needs her dad to walk her down the aisle. If you can pull all that off and still keep it a surprise, then we're ready to help!"

At the time Steve and I were under a pretty tight budget. He was working as a pastor in a small church, and we still had three children at home. But we had set aside $500 for Christmas, and we decided to use that money for the wedding.

Few people at our church had ever met Tony because he was away in the military when we came on staff. But when we told them about his idea to surprise Kylene with not only a proposal but also a wedding, they all got on board to help make it happen.

## SURPRISE WEDDING

Everyone waited in suspense to hear how Kylene responded to Tony's proposal and his idea to surprise her with a wedding. I went to a local hotel and told them Tony and Kylene's story. When I explained he was in the military and we were on a small budget, they gave me a great discount on the reception hall and on a room for the couple's wedding night.

A baker offered to make their wedding cake for the price of the ingredients when she heard Tony and Kylene's sweet love story. For decorations, the women in our church gathered lovely decor from their own homes, ready at a moment's notice to stage the ceremony and reception hall.

A dear family friend named Jackie offered to take their wedding photos for free. And another friend arranged for her two sons, who were accomplished violinists, to play music throughout the reception.

And the dress—oh, the dress! Tony had the idea to ask his biological sister, Elizabeth, if Kylene could borrow her wedding dress *if* she agreed to marry him. Tony's sister not only agreed, but she took on the task of covertly getting Kylene's measurements so she could have the gown altered to fit Kylene's tiny frame. And Elizabeth, who was living in England at the time, made plans to personally deliver the gown so she could be there for Tony and Kylene's wedding.

On the day Kylene flew into San Francisco, Tony had a lovely day planned, which included presenting her with a ring and asking her to be his wife. Kylene was completely taken by surprise when Tony popped the question. She began to rock back and forth, clutching her hands together as she asked Tony in her sweet southern accent, "Me? Are you sure you want to marry me?" (which, when I later heard her humble response to Tony's proposal, made me adore her).

When Tony assured Kylene of his love for her and his desire to make her his wife, she happily agreed as he slipped the beautiful engagement ring on her finger. As Kylene laughed and cried in utter joy, Tony held her in his arms.

After some time, he pulled away to ask her yet another question. "What if we get married this week?" Tony went on to outline his well-thought-out plan of presenting her with a surprise wedding, should she agree to the idea.

Without hesitation Kylene said, "Yes! Let's get married this week."

Our entire family had just sat down to dinner when Tony called home. "Code blue! Code blue! She said yes!" is what he shouted into the phone. We were all overjoyed with the news and immediately went into wedding-planning mode.

When Tony and Kylene finally arrived at our house, she couldn't help but be nervous about meeting his family. Her fears were short-lived as we all embraced her and told her she was the one we had been praying for God to send to Tony all these years.

Steve and I spent three days taking the couple through a premarital crash course that was ideally designed for six weeks of sessions. The team at church took care of the decorations and reception. Even though only a few of the church members had met Tony, their love for him and Kylene was a beautiful outpouring of Christ's love.

On the day of the wedding, Kylene and Tony's sisters were to get ready at the hotel room we reserved for their first night together. One of the young women at church was a hairdresser, and she volunteered to do Kylene's hair. Another did her makeup. And Kylene was overwhelmed when, prior to her getting ready, the young women of the church surprised her with an impromptu lingerie shower at the hotel room. Remember, Kylene came to California with no idea she would be getting married. So the girls reasoned she would need pretty lingerie for their honeymoon night.

## WEDDING ROMANCE

With Tony in his dress blue air force uniform and Kylene cascading down the aisle in that beautiful wedding gown, there wasn't a dry eye among us. The ceremony was beautiful, with Steve presenting the message of Christ's love for the church pictured in the marriage relationship.

At the reception, no one would ever have guessed the event had not taken months of planning and thousands of dollars. The romance of the evening climaxed when Tony and Kylene gazed into each other's eyes while waltzing to the violin playing "Could I Have This Dance for the Rest of My Life?"

After the traditional cake cutting and speeches, Tony took the microphone to thank everyone for their help in sweeping Kylene off her feet and surprising her with the wedding of her dreams. "We are amazed at the outpouring of your love for us. Y'all don't even know us and yet you did all of this to make Kylene's dream come true. We are forever grateful for your kindness and generosity."

With that, Tony took his bride by the hand and led her up the stairs to their honeymoon suite. When they arrived in the room, they found rose petals all over the floor and the bed, sparkling cider with fluted glasses, and a basket of wedding cards from the church family filled with money, gift cards, and notes of love and prayers for their marriage. Again, the two could hardly believe how blessed they had been.

Tony and Kylene had not had sex with each other before their wedding night, so the first night was most certainly going to be special. But what made it even more significant was that they would share only that one night together before Tony returned to work in Japan and Kylene flew back to Florida to finish her nursing degree.

You see, when Tony asked Kylene to marry him, one of the stipulations he put on her saying yes was that she had to promise him she would go back to complete the nursing degree she had worked so hard to obtain. The plan would be that Kylene would fly out to Japan for Christmas break and spring break, and then that summer, after she graduated nursing school, she would join Tony permanently in Japan.

## OCEANS APART

When Kylene agreed to Tony's plan, she had no idea how difficult it would be to keep her promise after spending only one night with him as his wife. The day after their wedding, Kylene pleaded with Tony to agree to her quitting nursing school and going with him. But after Tony's gentle reminder of how hard she had worked to get her degree, she reluctantly submitted.

Our hearts ached to watch the two say good-bye and part ways. Over the next several months, Kylene and I spent lots of time talking on the phone whenever she was feeling homesick for Tony or needing some motherly advice. Hearing how desperately she wanted to learn to be a godly wife to Tony caused my love for her to intensify.

When Kylene graduated from nursing school and joined Tony in Japan, the two were elated to finally begin living together as husband and wife. One day Tony called home and shared with us how deeply thankful he and Kylene had been for their lovely wedding. He said Kylene enjoyed telling anyone who would listen about that romantic surprise.

Tony and Kylene now have two precious children named Kelsey and William. They have been married for more than a decade, and they still love telling their wedding story. Since military life requires a lot of moving, Kylene's wedding gown hangs in a closet upstairs in our home. Perhaps one day her daughter will wear it. The dress is a sweet reminder of how God caused Tony to fall so deeply in love with the sweet southern girl he met on the beach that he couldn't wait one more day to make her his bride.

## PONDER THIS

Watching your children find their way is sometimes hard. As parents we want to be sure they never suffer any consequences for their mistakes. Watching and waiting for the Holy Spirit to guide our son Tony, rather than manipulating him toward what we wanted for his future, was not an easy task. But as we prayed and relied on God for His timing and direction for our boy, we had peace that the Holy Spirit would remind Tony of the purpose for which he was created and guide him to a wife who loved the Lord.

## ASK YOURSELF

When your kids are looking for love, you can find God's peace as you wait for Him to guide them by keeping your heart and mind focused on Christ. In times of worry my husband's mother often sang to us the old song, "Why Worry When You Can Pray?"

*Anxiety over a situation you cannot control will do nothing to help your children. But prayer is a force like none other.*

Rather than worrying or harping on your adult children when you want to help them, try asking God to bring to their remembrance the foundational truths they learned as young children. And if they did not grow up grounded in sound teaching, ask God to lead them to believers who will share Truth with them.

How might learning of Tony and Kylene's love story encourage you as a parent to pray more and manipulate less? Anxiety over a situation you cannot control will do nothing to help your children. But prayer is a force like none other. "Prayer is the most powerful tool we as parents have at our disposal."[1] So if you find yourself concerned over your children's pursuit of true love, share with them stories of God's faithfulness, and then pray like you've never prayed before for God to bring to them spouses who will love Jesus. And pray that God will use any means necessary to prepare your children to love with Christ's selfless love.

# 25

## Courageous Love

### The Apostle Peter and His Wife

I've been amazed at how much I've learned from the love stories in this book. How about you? I believe some people learn from others' successes and failures, but other people learn only from their own mistakes. I pray these love stories will help you be one who is inspired to grow more deeply in love with Jesus so His Spirit can grow you to love your husband with His perfect, selfless, wonderful love. (And if you are not yet married, I pray these stories will encourage you to wait on God for the man He will bring.)

Remember the couple you meant to be? The one you promised to be on the day you said "I do"? Take a moment to ponder how you're measuring up to your own expectations. What steps will you take to rekindle the love you have for your husband?

The Bible calls older women to teach younger women how to love their husbands and their children (Titus 2). My heart's mission as an author and speaker is to guide you toward a no-regrets life—to help you become the wife, mother, and woman you long to be.

Imagine if you had your own personal marriage mentor to help you build a no-regrets marriage. My husband, Steve, and I have written a new book that is just that—*The Marriage Mentor* (coming from Harvest House Publishers in 2018).

Through the pages of our book, Steve and I invite you to join us for more love stories and biblical guidance to help you become the couple you always meant to be—and have the marriage you long for.

This love story is an excerpt from the last chapter of *The Marriage Mentor*. I cannot get through this story without crying. But it also ignites a fire in my soul to have a marriage like the one reflected in the final moments between the apostle Peter and his wife.

—

Do you ever wonder what Peter's wife was thinking on the day her husband came home to announce he would be leaving the family fishing business to follow Jesus? Would this woman, who is unnamed in Scripture, have questioned Peter's decision to forsake all he had worked for to follow the One he believed was the Messiah? The Bible doesn't give us any insight into how Peter's conversion affected his marriage, but you can be sure that when I get to heaven I plan to find Peter's wife and ask her for the details of their story.

What very little we do know about Peter's wife includes the fact that Jesus healed her mother (Peter's mother-in-law) from a serious fever. Luke 4:39 (NKJV) tells us that "He stood over her and rebuked the fever, and it left her, and immediately she rose and began to serve them." We aren't told if Peter's wife witnessed this healing, but if she did, I would think this would have persuaded her to get behind her husband's decision to devote his life to following Jesus.

As we'll see in a moment, history reports that Peter's wife was a courageous follower of Jesus until her final breath. This dynamic couple must have been a powerful influence for the gospel at a time when Nero was persecuting Christians. At one point, when Peter was commanded to stop talking about Jesus, he responded, "We cannot but speak the things which we have seen and heard" (Acts 4:20 NKJV).

The commitment of Peter and his wife to boldly proclaim what they witnessed of Jesus's life, death, burial, and glorious resurrection would eventually cost them their lives. Eusebius, a well-learned Roman historian who lived from about AD 260 to 340, made this observation about the final moments between the apostle Peter and his beloved wife:

The blessed Peter, seeing his own wife led away to execution, was delighted, on account of her calling and return to her country, and that he cried to her in a consolatory and encouraging voice, addressing her by name: "Oh thou, remember the Lord!" Such was the marriage of these blessed ones.[1]

Can you imagine the final moment between Peter and his wife? How their eyes must have communicated volumes to each other as she was marched toward her execution? What courage she must have received to hear her sweet husband proclaim, "Remember the Lord!" as she was escorted along the path to her death. Did Peter's words remind her that in a few moments the Lord would be waiting to receive her into His kingdom?

*Have you ever considered that God brought you together with your husband because He has a mission for the two of you to accomplish—together?*

Peter and his wife were a powerful testimony for Christ to their generation. Do you realize the Lord wants to use you and your mate as a testimony to people as well? Have you ever considered that God brought you together with your husband because He has a mission for the two of you to accomplish—together?[2]

## PONDER THIS

*You are on a mission.* Every follower of Christ is called to reach people for God in their generation. We are to make God known, and to make Christ known so that people might come to redemption. As a Christian, anything you do in your life should be filtered through this missional statement: *To know Christ and make Him known.*

When you and your husband learn to live with a mission perspective, you will stop looking to each other to fix a difficult situation and turn to God instead. And you will trust that whatever trials or blessings God allows to come your way are divinely orchestrated by Him so "that you may be blameless and innocent, children of God without blemish in the midst of a crooked and twisted generation, among whom you shine as lights in the world" (Philippians 2:15 ESV). This allows God to use whatever means necessary to shine His glory through your obedient lives, so that through your testimony He creates an appetite in other people to know Christ.

To shine brightly means using your blessings to bless others, and always acknowledging that it is the Lord who provides—rather than taking the glory for your accomplishments. And it means walking through painful circumstances with joy so Christ's peace will shine brightly to everyone who is watching.

During nearly 35 years of marriage, Steve and I have experienced great blessings and deep sorrow. I am confident the Lord has more in store for us as we seek to serve Him and share the gospel with the people He brings across our paths. What about your marriage?

I challenge you to stop here and take a moment to ponder the highs and lows of your married life. Have you ever felt alone in the boat on a raging sea? How did you respond? Did you blame your husband for not making enough money, or not being sympathetic enough when you were hurting? Or maybe you have not yet gone through a truly painful experience. If so, I hate to break it to you, but you will. So rather than hope that will never happen, you would do well to begin growing your trust in the character of Christ through prayer and studying the Bible.

*When you read God's Word, ask Him to help you know Him better and trust Him more. Then you will be better prepared to not only survive life's storms, but to thrive in times of trouble.*

Through Scripture God has chosen to reveal to us His ways. When you read God's Word, ask Him to help you know Him better and trust Him more. Then you will be better prepared to not only survive life's storms, but to thrive in times of trouble.

## ASK YOURSELF

Do you live with a missional perspective? This means daily asking God to do those good works He planned to do through you before the foundation of this world (Ephesians 1:3-6; 2:10). When you wake up each day, ask God to give you a passion to seek His face through His Word so you can learn to trust Him more.

Will you courageously ask God to use every circumstance in your marriage to show others that a relationship with Christ is the only way to true happiness? Even if your husband does not keep his focus on Christ, when you do you can joyfully build a marriage that will grow stronger through life's blessings and sorrows—and God will be glorified.

## 26

# *One Last Love Story*

Throughout this book we have met couples who fell in love at first sight, found each other later in life, and grew more in love with each other through triumphs and trials. The final love story absolutely vital to completing this book is *your* love story!

If you're married, take some time to ponder how you and your spouse first met. Remember how you felt then, and then how you longed for him to return your affections. Remember how God providentially brought you together.

Imagine leaving your memoir for your grandchildren to read, and then write down your love story in a journal. This exercise will not only leave behind a glorious account for the next generation to read about how God knit together your heart with your love, but it will also serve as a reminder to you to grow your appreciation for your spouse. It will remind you what it is about him you fell in love with in the first place.

If you're not married, fill your pages with a prayer of commitment to wait upon the Lord to providentially bring to you a spouse, one He would have you walk with down the path where He will guide you. Include a prayer to remain sexually pure so that you can be sensitive to the leading of the Holy Spirit.

—

When our son Tony was in the ROTC at A&M University, he was the head of his unit. One woman under his command had a hard time keeping up with the men when they ran a great distance. When they arrived at their destination without her, they were chastised and required to do push-ups until she arrived. As commander, Tony needed to be sure she kept up the pace with the rest of the unit, so he ran in back alongside her. With both of their eyes focused on their destination, Tony would place his hand in the small of her back and she would keep up the pace. When he removed his hand, she lagged behind.

I tell this story at events for single women to show them a wonderful word picture. The Bible says that, as Christ followers, we're running a race He has set before us. He calls us to keep our eyes fixed on Him, the author and finisher of our faith, and to shake off whatever easily besets us in our pursuit to finish well.

*When looking for a mate, it's tempting to
take your eyes off the prize of Christ and
focus on who might be "the one."*

When looking for a mate, it's tempting to take your eyes off the prize of Christ and focus on who might be "the one." But let's follow the example of the woman in Tony's unit. If you run this race of life with your focus on the One who calls you to run, and one day you look over and see a man whose eyes are fixed on Jesus, and he places his hand in the small of your back to help you run your race—marry him! (And if you're a man, and you one day find your hand in the small of a woman's back, the back of a woman who runs with you, you might want to consider marrying her.)

## AND THEY ALL LIVED
## HAPPILY-EVER-AFTER

Happily-ever-after doesn't always end like the fairy tales. As we have seen in this book true happiness does not rest in a life without trouble. Rather, it comes when you discover the secret of finding your worth and joy in Christ alone. As you learn to pursue loving God first and foremost, your focus will be on Him and His plan for your life—rather than looking for happiness in how well you are loved by someone else. I pray God grants you true romance as Christ's love spills over into your own love story.

# *Epilogue*

After walking with you through these precious love stories I am sad our time together has come to an end. Remember to visit my website, NoRegretsWoman.com to watch or listen to couples share their love stories.

I'd love to connect with you, so please "like" my Facebook page: *Rhonda Stoppe No Regrets Woman* and let me know what God has taught you through these stories. You can also follow me on Instagram and Twitter @RhondaStoppe.

Jesus used storytelling as a powerful way to convey biblical truth. I believe these sweet love stories based in a biblical perspective have the power to rekindle romance in marriages, shine brightly God's plan for romance, and encourage those who are single to wait on the Lord to write their love stories. You can help me share this resource by posting on your favorite social media site a quote from the book and/or a picture of yourself with your copy of *Real Life Romance*.

# *How to Have a Relationship with Jesus*

*What on earth could she possibly mean by a relationship with Jesus?* I am so glad you want to know!

Did you know God created people so He could have a relationship with them? When the Lord created Adam and Eve and put them in the garden of Eden, He didn't leave them there with a list of religious rituals to perform while He observed from afar. No, Genesis 3:8 says God walked with Adam and Eve in the garden in the cool of the day. He spent time with them!

You have likely heard some form of the story of how God put a tree in the garden and commanded Adam and Eve not to eat of its fruit. If they did, He said, they would surely die (Genesis 2:17). Genesis 3 records how one day Satan tempted Eve to partake of the forbidden fruit. Eve, deceived and seduced by his lies, partook of the fruit. Adam followed suit. In the moment they disobeyed God's command, not only did their bodies begin to die physically, but, worse, God's Spirit left them and they died spiritually. Can you imagine how empty they must have felt when that happened?

You see, once Adam and Eve sinned, their souls belonged to Satan, and without someone to rescue them they were without hope of ever being in right standing with God again. God could no longer fellowship with them because they had sinned and were now sinful. Unless God provided a way, they and all mankind would be without hope of ever restoring their relationship with Him. Every one of us would be destined to spend eternity in hell, away from God's presence.

However, because of God's great love for His creation, He would make a way to rescue us and bring us back to Him. That's why we use the word *salvation*!

Have you ever wondered, *Why did God put that tree in the garden, anyway? I mean, if it wasn't there, Adam and Eve never would have been tempted.* Good question. One I have pondered myself.

I used to think that somehow Adam and Eve's sin caught God by surprise, so the Trinity—God the Father, God the Son, and God the Holy Spirit—entered into a holy huddle to figure out plan B for mankind's redemption. *Redemption* basically means "buy back." (See Revelation 5:9.)

I've since learned that God knew Adam and Eve would fall. Revelation 13:8 says Jesus was "slain from the foundation of the world." That means before God even created the world, or people, He knew they would need a Savior. And because of God's great love for mankind, and His desire to create people who could *choose* to love and serve Him, He put the tree in the garden to give Adam and Eve a choice. When they sinned, and He knew they would, God had already planned to offer up His Son to pay the price for their disobedience (Romans 5:12-21).

Imagine, God loved us so much that He sacrificed His only Son, and whoever believes in Him will not die but will live forever (John 3:16)! God says the very act of offering His greatest treasure, Jesus, was His way of showing you and me just how much He loves us. "God demonstrates His own love toward us, in that while we were still sinners, Christ died for us" (Romans 5:8). What an unbelievable way to show us how much He loves us.

So what does it mean to "believe in Him" like John 3:16 says? Is it a mere mental ascent to the truth that Jesus is fully God, and being fully God He took on the form of a man when He was born through a virgin? And that Jesus lived a sinless life and willingly gave Himself up to die a cruel death on a cross so that His blood (His sacrifice) would wash away our sins? And then He victoriously rose from the dead? While all those statements are true, if you simply *agree* with the facts about Jesus, that doesn't mean you have a relationship with Him. James 2:19 says even the demons believe, and they tremble in fear because they *know* who Jesus is and what He accomplished when He died for the sins of all people.

No, having a relationship with Jesus is entering into a personal covenant (or vow or promise) with Jesus. He wants us to make a lifelong commitment to Him. But how?

First, God wants you to repent of your sins. Repent means to agree with God that you're a sinner in need of a Savior, and that you have determined to turn away from your sins. The Bible says, "All have sinned and fall short of the glory of God" (Romans 3:23 ) and that only the blood of Jesus can wash away your sins (Hebrews 9:14).

I know it's easy to take offense when someone says, "You're a sinner." But let's be honest. You and I both know that although we try to do what's right, our natural instinct is to disobey God's laws. (Remember the Ten Commandments?)

You see, God gave us those laws *not* so we could try to become sinless by doing all that they command, but to show us that we'll *never* be able to measure up to the sinless life God requires to have a relationship with Him and enter into heaven when we die (Galatians 2:16; 3:24).

So where does that leave us? If Galatians 2:16 says, "A man is justified by the works of the law," then what can we do to please God? If He isn't watching to see if our good deeds outweigh our bad deeds by the time we die (a completely bogus concept that's not taught in Scripture), and if, as Romans 6:23 says, "the wages of sin is death," then how can we be rescued from judgment?

Again, I'm glad you asked! The Bible also says, "The gift of God is eternal life in Jesus Christ our Lord" and that we are justified (made right) "by faith in Christ" (Romans 6:23; Galatians 2:16 ).

The Bible teaches that Jesus is not one of the ways to salvation; He is the *only* way. In John 14:6 we're told Jesus said, "I am the way, the truth, and the life. No one comes to the Father except through Me." Those are Jesus's words, not mine. The *only* way to an intimate relationship with God is through Jesus. Only when we receive His free gift of salvation does Jesus's blood wash away all of our sins. God Himself said, "Though your sins are like scarlet, they shall be as white as snow" (Isaiah 1:18).

Think of it: God promises to wipe the slate completely clean! No matter how many bad decisions you've made up to this point, no matter how shameful your past, Jesus is offering you freedom from all of it! Freedom from the shame and the bondage of sin.

Once Jesus washes away your sins, He promises *never* to throw them in your face again. Psalm 103:12 in the Bible says, "as far as the east is from the west" is how far God removes our sins from us. (East never meets west, right? That means, in Christ our sins are taken away forever!)

But you don't get to just say some magic words like "I believe" and then go back to life as usual. Jesus says He wants you to surrender all that you are to Him. "If you confess with your mouth that Jesus is Lord [Master] and believe in your heart that God raised him from the dead, you will be saved" (Romans 10:9).

Jesus doesn't ask you to simply add Him onto your life. He wants to be your life. And to anyone who becomes Jesus's follower He promises He will give a new and pure heart. Second Corinthians 5:17 says, "If anyone is in Christ, he is a new creation; old things have passed away; behold, all things have become new" (ESV).

Believe me when I tell you that without a relationship with Jesus I was a selfish, arrogant, fearful, and materialistic woman. But when I accepted His free gift of salvation and surrendered my life to Him as my Lord, I was set free. I have never looked back! Jesus took the mess I was and gave me a new heart. Through Jesus, God forgave all my sins—*all* of them! And when I said yes to a relationship (there's that word again) with Jesus, He put within me His Holy Spirit. (So that's what was missing!) And God wants the same for you.

When God fills you with His Spirit, life makes sense! In fact, it's the life you were born to live, in fellowship with your creator. Nothing else in this life will ever satisfy your longing for Him—nothing.

If you enter into a relationship with Jesus, you never have to worry about being "good enough" for God to love you or let you into heaven when you die. To those who are in Christ, God says He adopts us as His very own children. "Behold what manner of love the Father has bestowed on us, that we should be called children of God" (1 John 3:1). Jesus says we can call God our Abba Father (Abba means "Daddy"). And God says His great love for us is perfect, immeasurable, and nothing we could ever do will make Him stop loving us! To top it off, God promises you will never be alone again. Jesus promises He will never leave you nor forsake you (Matthew 28:19-20; Hebrews 13:5). How awesome is that?

And there's one more thing. If you decide to believe Jesus died for you—*for you*—and you choose to agree with God that you need a Savior because of your sinful heart, and if you pray and submit to Jesus as the Lord of your life, then God's Spirit will fill your heart with His presence, peace, and purpose.

When you receive Jesus's free gift of salvation, He promises to lead you, guide you, and accomplish great things for His kingdom through your obedient life, for the rest of your life. Ephesians 2:8-10 says, "By grace [that means you can't earn it] you have been saved through faith, and that not of yourselves; it is the gift of God, not of works, lest anyone should boast. For [you] are His workmanship, created in Christ Jesus for good works, which God prepared beforehand." God has a plan for your life. Isn't that exciting?

Now you know what it means to have a relationship with Jesus. It's my prayer that the Holy Spirit is drawing you to Christ even at this moment, and that you will pray to receive Jesus as your Lord and Savior so you can begin this wonderful journey of walking with Him for the rest of your life—and on into heaven in the next!

## About Rhonda

Rhonda Stoppe is the No Regrets Woman. *"I could have listened to Rhonda talk all night,"* is what women say about Rhonda's enthusiastic, genuine, and transparent style of teaching. Through humor and honest communication, she helps women build NO REGRETS LIVES by teaching them how to apply sound teaching from the Bible to all issues of life. With more than 30 years of experience as a pastor's wife, mom, mentor, author, and speaker, Rhonda has helped women to

- discover significance and purpose for their lives
- enjoy a marriage others only dream about
- impact the moral fiber of the next generation by raising children with integrity
- find victory over people-pleasing
- parent without regrets
- build an incredible legacy
- become more influential than they ever dreamed possible

Rhonda has appeared on numerous radio programs including *Family Life Today* & *Family Talk* with Dr. James Dobson, and she is a favorite speaker at women's events, MOPs, and homeschool conventions, and on college campuses.

For free resources and to book Rhonda for your next event, visit her at **NoRegretsWoman.com**.

To learn more about Rhonda Stoppe or to read sample chapters, visit our website at **www.harvesthousepublishers.com**.

To learn more about Harvest House books and
to read sample chapters, log on to our website:

**www.harvesthousepublishers.com**

HARVEST HOUSE PUBLISHERS
EUGENE, OREGON